LOCKHEED
SKUNK WORKS

Steve Pace

Motorbooks International
Publishers & Wholesalers ®

First published in 1992 by Motorbooks International Publishers & Wholesalers, PO Box 2, 729 Prospect Avenue, Osceola, WI 54020 USA

Motorbooks International books are also available at discounts in bulk quantity for industrial or sales-promotional use. For details write to Special Sales Manager at the Publisher's address

Library of Congress Cataloging-in-Publication Data
Pace, Steve.
   Lockheed Skunk Works
 / Steve Pace.
       p. cm.
   Includes index.
   ISBN 0-87938-632-0
 1. Lockheed Advanced Development Company—History.
 2. Aeronautics—Research—United States—History. I. Title.
 TL565.P33   1992
 629.13′0072073—dc20   92-28518

On the front cover: A Lockheed cutaway drawing showing the internal structure of the F-117A. *Lockheed*

On the back cover: Top, Clarence L. ("Kelly") Johnson, the founder of the Skunk Works, poses with one of his most famous creations, the U-2 spyplane, which became infamous when one was shot down over the Soviet Union on 1 May 1960. Center, Benjamin R. ("Ben") Rich succeeded Kelly Johnson as "Chief Skunk" in 1975. He poses here with the SR-71 Blackbird, one of the many ground-breaking aircraft he helped design. Bottom, Sherman N. ("Sherm") Mullin succeeded Ben Rich in 1990. Mullin led the Lockheed-Boeing-General Dynamic team that won the US Air Force demonstration and validation program for the YF-22A, which will replace the F-15 as the US Air Force's air superiority fighter. *Lockheed*

On the frontispiece: Lockheed's Skunk Works air vehicle production facility: Site 2 at U.S. Air Force Plant 42, Palmdale, California. This is where Lockheed aircraft such as the U-2R, A-12, F-12, SR-71, Have Blue XST, and F-117 were built. The one-of-a-kind A-12T *Titanium Goose*, two U-2s, and three SR-71s are shown. *Lockheed Advanced Development Company; Denny Lombard*

Printed and bound in the United States of America

Contents

	Acknowledgments	7
Chapter 1	Lockheed Advanced Development Company: The Skunk Works	9
Chapter 2	Concepts and Images	31
Chapter 3	F-80 Shooting Star	39
Chapter 4	T-33 T-Bird and T-1A SeaStar	55
Chapter 5	F-94 Starfire	66
Chapter 6	XF-90 Penetration Fighter	85
Chapter 7	X-7 and XQ-5 King Fisher	96
Chapter 8	XF-104 Starfighter	104
Chapter 9	XFV-1 Salmon	113
Chapter 10	YC-130 Hercules	121
Chapter 11	JetStar	126
Chapter 12	U-2 Dragon Lady	130
Chapter 13	A-12 Blackbird and D-21 Drone	153
Chapter 14	YF-12 Blackbird	183
Chapter 15	SR-71 Blackbird	196
Chapter 16	XST	219
Chapter 17	F-117A Black Jet	227
Chapter 18	F-22 Lightning II	254
	Postscript	276
	Bibliography	284
	Index	285

*This book is dedicated to all past, present, and future
employees of Lockheed's Skunk Works, in
appreciation for helping to keep the free world strong
through air power with your many advanced
development projects for a half century.*

Acknowledgments

I greatly appreciate the contributions made to this reference by the following: Rich Stadler, Denny Lombard, and Jim Ragsdale, Lockheed Advanced Development Company; Eric Schulzinger, Roy Blay, and April McKettrick, Lockheed Corporation; Jeff Rhodes, Lockheed Aeronautical Systems Company; Tony LeVier, Skunk Works pilot, retired; Ben Rich, Skunk Works president, retired; Jim Young and Cheryl Gumm, Air Force Flight Test Center History Office; Don Nolan, NASA Ames-Dryden Flight Research Facility public affairs office; Tony Landis, Mach 3–plus aviation photographer; Mike Machat; Jim Goodall; and Greg Field, Barbara Harold, Mary LaBarre, and the rest of the fine editorial staff at Motorbooks International publishing.

Chapter 1

Lockheed Advanced Development Company: The Skunk Works

The Skunk Works is a concentration of a few good people solving problems far in advance—and at a fraction of the cost—by applying the simplest, most straightforward methods possible to develop and produce new products.

—Kelly Johnson

In aerospace, Lockheed's top-secret Skunk Works has been a bona fide success for almost a half century. Since mid-1943, it has produced for the U.S. Armed Forces, intelligence agencies, and the National Aeronautics and Space Administration (NASA) a series of advanced aircraft for combat, transport, reconnaissance, and research.

The mission of Lockheed Advanced Development Company—the Skunk Works—is to satisfy any national need for prototyping or specialized technology to produce a limited quantity of rapidly required aircraft in a quick, quiet, and cost-effective manner using all the strengths of Lockheed Corporation.

Although initially shrouded in secrecy, many of the aircraft developed in the Skunk Works have become aviation legends. Included are the F-80 Shooting Star, which in 1950, achieved fame as the first aircraft to win an all-jet aerial battle when it downed a Soviet-built MiG-15 during the Korean War; the U-2 reconnaissance aircraft, still the world's highest-altitude single-engine jet at more than 70,000 feet (ft); the record-setting F-104 Starfighter, the first doublesonic aircraft; the SR-71 Blackbird, which initially flew in 1964 but still holds the world aircraft marks for speed (more than 2,200 miles per hour [mph]) and altitude (85,000 feet plus); and the F-117A stealth fighter, the first operational

9

Sherman N. ("Sherm") Mullin, president of Lockheed Advanced Development Company—the Skunk Works. Lockheed

aircraft designed for low observability, whose Lockheed–U.S. Air Force development team won the 1989 Collier Trophy.

The birth of what soon was nicknamed the Skunk Works took place in June 1943 when the U.S. Army Air Forces asked Lockheed to design a fighter around a British de Havilland turbojet engine in the wake of the disturbing news that the Nazis had already flown their own 500mph jet fighter in the skies over Europe; under an agreement negotiated by Chief Research Engineer Clarence L. ("Kelly") Johnson, Lockheed was to deliver a prototype XP-80 airplane within only six months.

With the approval of President Robert E. Gross of Lockheed, Johnson pirated personnel from other wartime projects. He forged a team of twenty-seven other engineers and 105 shop mechanics working in a small assembly shed near the Lockheed wind tunnel at Burbank, California. The Skunk Works, founded by Johnson, completed the first XP-80—dubbed *Lulu-Belle*—in 143 days, thirty-seven days under schedule. The prototype jet fighter, which made its first flight in January 1944 at Rogers Dry Lake (now part of Edwards Air Force Base, which was formerly Muroc Army Air Field), California, was the forerunner of the classic F-80 Shooting Star, America's first operational jet fighter.

Origin of the Skunk Works Name

The formal name for the Skunk Works for many years was Advanced Development Projects. In 1990, Advanced Development Projects was converted into a separate Aeronautical Systems Group division: Lockheed Advanced Development Company.

The name Skunk Works came from Al Capp's *Li'l Abner* comic strip, which featured the "skonk works," where Appalachian hillbillies ground up skunks, old shoes, and other foul-smelling ingredients to brew fearsome drinks and other products.

To hide its true nature, Lockheed engineers identified the secret XP-80 assembly shed—which ironically was across the street from a malodorous plastics factory—as the place where Kelly Johnson was stirring up some kind of potent brew. The nickname stuck, although *skonk* became *skunk* in deference to the nonhillbillies working at the top-secret facility and because Capp objected to anyone else using his unique spelling.

Cartoonist Capp and his *Li'l Abner* comic strip departed many years ago, but the Skunk Works—a registered service mark of Lockheed Corporation along with the familiar skunk logo—lives on as Lockheed Advanced Development Company continues to "brew" the world's most potent aircraft.

The Lockheed F-22, powered by two Pratt & Whitney F119 engines, is to be the advanced tactical fighter of the future. The Pratt & Whitney YF119– powered YF-22—winner of the advanced tactical fighter competition—is shown. Lockheed

At first, Johnson did not like the Skunk Works name at all. In fact, he wanted to dismiss it altogether. But as time went by, more and more secret aircraft projects came into being, and the nickname began to take on a character all its own. Finally, Johnson accepted it as appropriate.

Kelly Johnson: Skunk Works' Creator

The achievements of Kelly Johnson, the aeronautical wizard who created Lockheed's supersecret Skunk Works and designed the world's fastest and highest-flying aircraft, made him an aerospace legend.

Johnson died on 21 December 1990, honored by America and by the aerospace community for his outstanding and innovative contributions in advancing aviation and safeguarding the free world.

Johnson's achievements go back to the 1930s, but he may be best remembered for organizing the Lockheed Skunk Works in 1943. It started as a small unit of engineering and production specialists to hurriedly create, build, and fly the World War II XP-80 jet fighter prototype for the U.S. Army Air Forces.

The XP-80 was just the first of many of the world's most advanced aircraft to be produced by the Skunk Works under his leadership.

Born in Ishpeming, Michigan, on 27 February 1910, Clarence

Johnson received his nickname of Kelly in elementary school from a popular song of the day, "Kelly from the Emerald Isle." His classmates figured that someone who licked the school bully should be known by a somewhat more pugilistic name than Clarence. The nickname stayed with him from that point on—and he never backed away from controversy on aircraft design, materials, and production techniques.

Johnson joined Lockheed in Burbank in 1933 as an $83-a-month tool designer after receiving a master's degree in aeronautical engineering from the University of Michigan, working his way through college with the aid of some grants. Johnson had earlier impressed Lockheed management as a graduate student when he tested examples of the proposed Lockheed Model 10 Electra transport in the university's wind tunnel and suggested significant design changes.

Five years after joining Lockheed, Johnson was named the company's chief research engineer. He became chief engineer in 1952 and corporate vice-president for research and development in 1956.

Even as he advanced in management, Johnson continued as a creator of innovative aircraft. He designed the twin-boom P-38 Lightning—the "Fork-tailed Devil," as Germany dubbed it in World War II—and was instrumental in converting the commercial Lockheed Model 14 Super Electra into the celebrated Hudson bomber.

Johnson played a leading role in the design of more than forty other aircraft, including the triple-tail Constellation transport, the P-2 Neptune antisubmarine patrol plane, the record-setting F-104 Starfighter, the U-2 reconnaissance aircraft, and the SR-71 Blackbird, the world's fastest jet aircraft.

He was also sent to Lockheed Missiles and Space Company in the San Francisco Bay area to set up a Skunk Works–type operation to develop the Agena-D satellite, which became the nation's workhorse in space.

Johnson became known for his strict adherence to principles. On several occasions, he turned back development contracts to the U.S. Department of Defense (DOD) after initial work indicated the proposed aircraft would not be effective, no matter how much money the Department of Defense was willing to provide. He also returned to the U.S. government approximately $2 million on a $20 million U-2 contract after building twenty-six aircraft for the same money intended to cover twenty aircraft.

Dubbed Lulu-Belle, the XP-80 as it originally appeared after its arrival at the North Base Area of Muroc Army Air Base, California, in January 1944. As the first official creation of Lockheed's Skunk Works, the XP-80 formed the matrix that molded a number of winning designs that included the T-33 and the F-94. Lockheed

The second of two XF-104 prototypes. Appearing publicly for the first time in 1956—some two years after its first flights—the missilelike Lockheed F-104 Starfighter was the world's fastest and most advanced fighter. Lockheed

He won every major aircraft design award in the industry, some for the second and third time. Included were two Collier Trophies, two Theodore von Karman Awards, the Wright Brothers Memorial Trophy, two Sylvanus Albert Reed Awards, and the Daniel Guggenheim Medal. In 1964, President Lyndon Johnson presented him the nation's highest civilian honor, the Medal of Freedom. President Ronald Reagan honored him with the National Security Medal in 1983 and the National Medal of Technology in 1988. Johnson was enshrined in the Aviation Hall of Fame in 1983, and during the same year, he was featured on the *60 Minutes* television program.

He was also honored by his employer in 1983, when Lockheed Corporation renamed its Rye Canyon, California, facility the Kelly Johnson Research and Development Center.

In the Lockheed pamphlet *This Is . . . LADC*, Johnson was described by Senator Sam Nunn as a "truly unique national asset" and by former deputy defense secretary David Packard as a "national treasure."

President Johnson, presenting the National Medal of Science to Kelly Johnson, noted: "Kelly Johnson and the products of his famous Skunk Works epitomize the highest and finest goal of our society—the goal of excellence. His record of design achievement in aviation is both incomparable and virtually incredible. Any one of his many airplane designs would have honored any individual's career."

Kelly Johnson retired from Lockheed in 1975 as a corporate senior vice president. He resigned from the corporation's board of directors in 1980 but continued to serve as a senior advisor until his death.

In 1985, his autobiography, *Kelly: More Than My Share of It All*, was published by the Smithsonian Institution. Said Kelly Johnson, summing it up, "I consider myself very fortunate to have lived my professional life doing exactly what I always wanted to do."

Ben Rich: Lockheed Advanced Development Company's First President

When the new Lockheed Advanced Development Company was formed in May 1990 from the former Advanced Development Projects organization—the Skunk Works—Benjamin R. (Ben) Rich was named the company's first president and dubbed Chief Skunk.

Ben Rich planned to become a medical doctor, but a career detour eventually took him to Lockheed in 1950 as an aeronautical engineer, and then in 1954, to the Skunk Works where he cured problems in the design of advanced aircraft.

Rich participated in the thermodynamics, propulsion, and preliminary design aspects of the F-104; the U-2; the Blackbird series of A-12, YF-12, and SR-71 aircraft; and the D-21 drone. He joined the SR-71 program in its beginning A-1 through A-12 phases in 1958 as an aerothermodynamic engineer. At his suggestion, the triplesonic A-12, YF-12, and SR-71 aircraft were painted black to reduce the searing temperatures on it.

By 1963, he was senior engineer for advanced programs. Nine years later, Rich had advanced to vice-president for fighter programs and preliminary designs.

In 1975, Ben Rich succeeded Kelly Johnson as a company vice-president and general manager of the Skunk Works, a job he held until 1990, except for a 1984–86 interim assignment as president of the Lockheed Advanced Aeronautics Company. Rich became a Lockheed corporate vice-president in 1977.

After retiring in December 1990 following a forty-year Lockheed career, Rich continues to

An early U-2A of the 4080th Strategic Reconnaissance Wing. First flown in August 1955, the Lockheed U-2 is still a successful aerial reconnaissance platform. Lockheed

be of service to Lockheed Advanced Development Company and the corporation as a consultant.

Leading the development of the F-117A stealth fighter, Rich won the 1989 Collier Trophy in association with the entire Lockheed-U.S. Air Force team responsible for the success of this aircraft program.

A fellow of the American Institute of Aeronautics and Astronautics, Rich received the institute's national aircraft design award in 1972.

In 1988, he was selected the Wright Brothers annual lecturer by both the American Institute of Aeronautics and Astronautics and the British Royal Aeronautical Society. In January 1991, following his retirement from Lockheed, Rich was elected an honorary fellow of the American Institute of Aeronautics and Astronautics.

Rich was elected to the National Academy of Engineering in 1981 and in 1982, was named Alumnus Engineer of the Year at the University of California at Los Angeles, where he received his master's degree in engineering. He received his bachelor's degree from the University of California at Berkeley.

Rich, the son of British subjects, was born on 18 June 1925 in Manila, the Philippine Islands. Exactly fifty-six years later, on 18 June 1981, the premier F-117A made its first flight.

Sherm Mullin: Lockheed Advanced Development Company's Second President

Sherman N. ("Sherm") Mullin succeeded Ben Rich as Chief Skunk and president of Lockheed Advanced Development Company in December 1990. He formerly headed up the F-22 advanced tactical fighter program as vice-president and general manager of the team program office. As a Lockheed Aeronautical Systems Company vice-president and general manager for the advanced tactical fighter program, Mullin led the Lockheed–Boeing–General Dynamics team that won a U.S. Air Force demonstration and validation contract for the YF-22A prototype program on 31 October 1986. The Lockheed F-22 advanced tactical fighter was developed by Lockheed Aeronautical Systems Company with the assistance of many key engineers from the Skunk Works, and on 23 April 1991, the YF-22A prevailed over its Northrop–McDonnell Douglas YF-23A competition.

Mullin joined Lockheed Electronics Company in 1959 as an electronics engineer. Transferring to Lockheed-California Company in 1968, he played a major role in the advanced systems and computer software incorporated in the P-3 Orion and S-3 Viking antisubmarine warfare aircraft. He was promoted to chief engineer on the P-3 program in 1974. He was

Undoubtedly, the Skunk Works' greatest accomplishment was its unparalleled SR-71 Blackbird. Now retired from active U.S. Air Force duty, the triplesonic-plus-speed SR-71 set the standard by which all exotic aircraft—past, present, and future—can be judged. Tony Landis

21

P-3 program manager from 1976 to 1980 and was director of planning and advanced programs in 1981 and 1982. In 1982, he was named vice-president of the Skunk Works and was assigned as program manager on the F-117A stealth fighter program.

Mullin was elected a Lockheed corporate vice-president in 1988. He is an associate fellow of the American Institute of Aeronautics and Astronautics, a senior member of the Institute of Electrical and Electronics Engineers, and a member of the American Association of the Advancement of Science. Born in Somers, Connecticut, on 12 October 1935, Mullin attended Princeton and other universities. He completed the Stanford Executive Program in 1984.

Sherm Mullin described the Skunk Works and its mission in the Lockheed brochure *This Is . . . LADC:*

All of us at LADC—the Skunk Works, have a vital role in protecting our nation. We design, develop, build and fly the world's most advanced aircraft in defense of the United States of America and its people.

Since the World War II founding of the Lockheed Skunk Works almost a half-century ago by Clarence L. (Kelly) Johnson, our organization has produced such outstanding aircraft as:

- America's first operational jet fighter plane—the F-80 Shooting Star, evolving from the 1943 XP-80 prototype
- The first operational fighter plane capable of flying twice the speed of sound—the F-104 Starfighter, evolving from the 1954 XF-104 prototype
- Advanced reconnaissance and research aircraft, typified by the U-2 and the SR-71
- The world's first operational stealth aircraft, the F-117A
- And many other high technology aerospace vehicles

Most were developed in secret by the Skunk Works. The safeguarding of classified information has long been a Skunk Works hallmark.

The creativity and achievements of the Skunk Works have been commended by the U.S. government and have triggered laudatory articles in business and aerospace magazines and have been praised in management books. The Lockheed-registered "Skunk Works" name even has its own definition in the Random House dictionary: "Often a secret experimental division, laboratory, or project for producing innovative design or products in the computer or aerospace field."

The basic philosophy of the Skunk Works comes from the engineering and management genius of Kelly Johnson. The message to LADC employees is brief and valuable:
- Deal only from absolute truth and honesty—with your customer, co-workers, our subcontractors and yourself.
- Live by Kelly Johnson's fourteen operating rules [listed

in the next section of this chapter]—they are not a passing fad.

• Establish a legacy of the highest ethical standards and performance excellence—it will live on after your time.

• Give your people a job to do and let them do it—you'll be happily surprised at the results.

We have a great legacy.

We have a challenging future.

We have an important job to do.

We will build our future together.

Sherm Mullin
President, Lockheed Advanced Development Company

Kelly Johnson's Basic Operating Rules for the Skunk Works:

1. The Skunk Works manager must be delegated practically complete control of his program in all respects. He should report to a division president or higher.
2. Strong but small project offices must be provided by both the military and industry.
3. The number of people having any connection with the project must be restricted in an almost vicious manner. Use a small number of good people (ten to twenty-five percent compared to the so-called normal systems).
4. A very simple drawing and drawing release system with great flexibility for making changes must be provided.
5. There must be a minimum of reports required, but important work must be recorded thoroughly.
6. There must be a monthly cost

review covering not only what has been spent and committed but also projected costs to the conclusion of the program. Don't have the books ninety days late and don't surprise the customer with sudden overruns.

7. The contractor must be delegated—and must assume more than normal responsibility—to get good vendor bids on the project. Commercial bid procedures are very often better than military ones.

8. The inspection system as currently used by LADC, which has been approved by both the U.S. Air Force and U.S. Navy, meets the intent of existing military requirements and should be used on new projects. Push more basic inspection responsibility back to subcontractors and vendors. Don't duplicate so much inspection.

9. The contractor must be delegated the authority to test his final product in flight. If he doesn't, he rapidly loses his competency to design other vehicles.

10. The specifications applying to the hardware must be agreed to in advance of contracting. The ADP [now Lockheed Advanced Development Company] practice of having a specification section stating clearly which important military specification items will not be knowingly complied with and reasons therefore is highly recommended.

11. Funding a program must be timely so that the contractor doesn't have to keep running to the bank to support government projects.

12. There must be mutual trust

between the military project organization and the contractor, with very close cooperation and liaison on a day-to-day basis. This cuts down misunderstanding and correspondence to an absolute minimum.

13. Access by outsiders to the project and its personnel must be strictly controlled by appropriate security measures.

14. Because only a few people will be used in engineering and most other areas, ways must be provided to reward good performance by pay not based on the number of personnel supervised.

What LADC Means: Quick . . . Quiet . . . Cost-effective . . .

Quality

What LADC employees stand for:

INTEGRITY—Personal and professional.

TEAMWORK—We work together to solve problems. We keep the team small; choose a few good people and give them the authority to do the job.

ATTITUDE—We take pride in our work. We will meet the customer's needs by delivering high-quality products.

COMMUNICATIONS—We are timely, open and honest with customers and co-workers. Important decisions are recorded but with minimum paperwork.

Both a workhorse and star of Operation Desert Storm, the Lockheed F-117A stealth fighter epitomized the meaning   *of precision bomb strikes when needed. Lockheed; Eric Schulzinger; Denny Lombard*

PROFIT—We watch costs and give the Lockheed shareholder a good return.

SECURITY—We comply with the strictest requirements. We are constantly aware of maintaining tight security.

CREATIVITY—We are constantly looking for better solutions. We seek technical innovations. We identify problems early and solve them.

SAFETY/HEALTH—We provide a safe and healthy workplace. We believe in a drug-free workforce.

PERFORMANCE—We produce products that perform as intended. We deliver on time and within budget.

QUALITY—We build in quality starting with the design team. Employees inspect their own work. We take pride in the quality of our products.

Skunk Works Leadership

In its corporate code of ethics, *The Lockheed Way*, Lockheed affirms its commitment to manage its employees effectively and equitably—respecting their dignity, encouraging their professional growth and advancement, and providing a healthy work environment characterized by open communication. The following guidelines, rooted in the corporate commitment and in historic Skunk Works values and beliefs, have been adopted by Lockheed Advanced Development Company senior management. They outline the specific types of action required to translate Lockheed's commitment into reality. At one level, they express the responsibilities of supervisors and managers, describing the type of behavior that employees have a right to expect from their management. At a deeper level, these guidelines sum up the obligations of every member of the Skunk Works family: the mutual respect, communication, and teamwork that will ensure Lockheed Advanced Development Company's success into the future.

Respect the Dignity of Each Employee

1. Act in a professional manner at all times. Treat each employee with respect and dignity.
2. Be courteous and consistent in your treatment of employees.
3. Encourage your employees' ideas and suggestions.
4. Treat your employees as you would want to be treated; maintain an atmosphere free of harassment or discrimination.
5. Use discretion when counseling. Counsel in private; praise in public.
6. Assist employees in their responsibility for career development; make them aware of opportunities and alternate career paths.

Recognize and Reward Performance

7. Openly recognize employees who excel: give awards, letters of appreciation and certificates of achievement. Recognize nonperformance and take appropriate corrective action promptly.
8. Ensure that salary increases

Robert E. Gross, former president of Lockheed Aircraft Corporation, gave his permission to Clarence L. ("Kelly") Johnson in mid-1943 to pirate 27 engi- neers and 105 shop mechanics from other projects to form the original Skunk Works. Lockheed

are fair and given on the basis of performance.

Provide a Safe and Healthy Workplace

9. Reinforce safety consciousness through regular staff or safety meetings.

10. Conduct regular safety and housekeeping inspections and take corrective action as required.

11. Train new employees on health and safety concerns in your area; be sure employees understand the safe use of hazardous and toxic chemicals.

Promote Employee Integrity

12. Set an example of integrity by your own conduct.

13. Promote Lockheed principles of ethics at staff meetings.

14. Demand strict adherence to labor recording requirements.

Strive for Two-way Communication with Employees

15. Hold regular staff meetings to ensure that your employees are kept informed.

16. Manage by "walking around" to encourage direct communication with your employees.

17. Listen to your employees and provide them with timely feedback on their suggestions and questions.

18. Communicate LADC goals to all employees.

Kelly Johnson, founder of Lockheed's Skunk Works, sat in the back seat of the tandem-seat A-12 for the first ride in what was to become his ultimate creation: the Blackbird series of aircraft. Lockheed

Lockheed's former Rye Canyon Research Laboratory near Valencia, California. The facility was renamed the Kelly Johnson Research and Development Center on 8 June 1983 to commemorate Johnson's 50 years of service to Lockheed as the firm's greatest aircraft designer. In part, it consists of the following structures: Weapon System Simulation Center; Supersonic Wind Tunnel; Hypersonic, Hypervelocity, and Propulsion Tunnels; Aerospace Environments Laboratory; Electromagnetics Laboratory; Composite Materials Laboratory; Thermal Systems Laboratory; Acoustics Laboratory; Fatigue and Fracture Mechanics Laboratory; and 11 other laboratories designed for vehicle systems, structures, and materials research. Lockheed

Benjamin R. ("Ben") Rich, the first president of Lockheed Advanced Devel- *opment Company, poses with a Black-bird that he helped to create. Lockheed*

19. Involve employees in team-building, problem solving, and—to the extent possible—decision making.
20. Ensure that employee concerns are communicated to senior management clearly and promptly and without "filtering." Bad news must get to the top as quickly as good news.
21. Encourage employees to identify causes of waste, recommend improvements in their work process, and implement changes.
22. Train employees in the basic problem-solving skills they can use to make quality and productivity improvements.
23. Give employees assignments and training to broaden their skills and understanding.
24. Give employees honest and frequent feedback on their performance—both strengths and weaknesses.
25. Expect the most from your employees and give them recognition when they perform as expected.

Onward and Upward

On 21 November 1991, Lockheed's Skunk Works announced plans to relocate its headquarters and most of the other remaining Burbank operations to Palmdale, California.

According to the November 1991 *LADC Information Sheet*, President Sherm Mullin of the Skunk Works said the company will construct a 300,000 square foot office building at its existing Palmdale facility to accommodate most of the moving functions. Some others will be housed in existing or leased buildings or both. He also said,

"Assuming we are able to make satisfactory arrangements with appropriate governmental agencies, this will permit us to continue our progress in relocating LADC's base of operations to Palmdale."

"This is the next phase of the restructuring plan we began in April 1989," Mullin said. "It will not only complete consolidation of most of our operations, but it will also give us modern factory, office, and laboratory facilities comparable to any in the aerospace industry."

Although the number of employees affected at the time will depend on the programs on hand at Lockheed Advanced Development Company, Mullin said the new building will house approximately 1,300 people. Plans call for the building to be completed in mid-1993—the Skunk Works' fiftieth anniversary—and fully occupied by December 1993.

Chapter 2

Concepts and Images

The *Skunk Works,* a copyrighted tradename, will be now separately
incorporated—although wholly owned by Lockheed Corporation. The
organizational philosophy will continue and its project mix, largely
classified, remains our business goal for the organization. The Skunk
Works enterprise style is universally applauded and copied around the
world.

—Ken Cannestra

In mid-1939, four years before the
official establishment of the Skunk
Works organization by Kelly
Johnson, Lockheed management
opted to funnel company funds
into hush-hush projects in hope of
generating business. To start,
Lockheed management directed
Chief Propulsion Engineer Nathan
C. ("Nate") Price to design, develop,
and run an advanced type of
aircraft propulsion unit: a gas
turbine, or turbojet, engine.

Under strict security
measures, Price formed a select
group of propulsion technicians,
established a secret shop, and went
to work on what the group thought
would be the first turbojet engine
in America—indeed, the world.
Unknown to them at the time,
however, Germany and England
were also designing and
developing their own versions of
jet propulsion units. In fact,
Germany was on the verge of
flight-testing the Heinkel He 178,
powered by a single Heinkel-Hirth
HeS3B engine, which made its first
official flight on 27 August 1939.
At the time, though, Price and his
colleagues did not even know if the
creation of such a powerplant was
possible. Nonetheless, they
proceeded with their work as if
they were exclusive to this type of
powerplant design and
development.

Temporary Design Number
L-1000

Lockheed's secret organization
issued Temporary Design Number

L-1000 to the turbojet engine design. Under the direction of Chief Engineer Hall L. Hibbard of Lockheed, Price and his associates completed the design of Temporary Design Number L-1000 in late 1941. It featured a number of extremely advanced characteristics such as a high compression ratio, twin-spool turbine stages, axial flow, an afterburning section, and a lower specific fuel consumption than that of its centrifugal-flow contemporaries. At the time, however, Price and his teammates had no idea just how advanced their version of a jet engine was. Even its uninstalled static sea level thrust rating of 5,500 pounds with afterburning was unheard of.

Nathan C. ("Nate") Price, shown at right with Hall L. Hibbard, headed the design of Lockheed's L-1000 (XJ37) axial-flow turbojet engine. Lockheed

Lockheed secretly submitted its L-1000 turbojet engine design to the U.S. Army Air Forces Air Materiel Command (AMC) at Wright Army Air Field (AAF) (redesignated Wright-Patterson Air Force Base on 13 January 1948), Dayton, Ohio, on an unsolicited basis in January 1942. Simultaneously, Lockheed submitted an unsolicited airframe design—an advanced fighter—to employ its new propulsion system, designated in-house Temporary Design Number L-133. Both proposals were well received, especially the turbojet engine, and Lockheed was instructed to wait for specific instructions on their respective futures. At the time, Lockheed was not told of current jet airframe and powerplant developments in the United States and abroad. Worse, both projects were all but being ignored.

Temporary Design Number L-133

During 1941, since Lockheed had designed and was developing what it believed was the world's first turbojet engine, it naturally designed an airframe to utilize it: the Lockheed Temporary Design Number L-133, a fighter plane.

To accomplish this, Chief Engineer Hall Hibbard and Assistant Chief Engineer Kelly Johnson formed a secret preliminary design team and went to work. Their immediate goal was to design a single-seat, twin-engine

Hall L. Hibbard, Lockheed's chief engineer. Lockheed

fighter with matchless performance.

What Hibbard, Johnson, and their co-workers came up with was a radical departure from the norm as far as fighter types go. In their attempt to combat aerodynamic heating because of the fighter's projected top speed of 600 plus, the aircraft was to be constructed of stainless steel. It featured tricycle landing gear (relatively new at the time), a canard foreplane, four nose-mounted 20 millimeter cannons, and an engine air inlet and ducting system in the nose section. But its major selling point—albeit for nothing, as it turned out—was its fantastic performance projections. These included the following:

- Top speed at sea level—615 miles per hour
- Top speed at 20,000 feet—620 miles per hour
- Top speed at 40,000 feet—602 miles per hour
- Maximum takeoff run distance to clear a 50 foot high object—1,885 feet
- Maximum climb rate at sea level—3,740 feet per minute
- Maximum climb rate at 20,000 feet—5,670 feet per minute
- Maximum climb rate at 40,000 feet—6,350 feet per minute

Lockheed's proposed L-133 stainless steel fighter of 1942. With its canard foreplanes and projected speed of more than 700 miles per hour, one wonders why it wasn't accepted for development. Lockheed

● Minimum time to climb to 40,000 feet—7.3 minutes
● Terminal dive speed at sea level—710 miles per hour
● Normal range at sea level—320 miles; at 20,000 feet—350 miles; and at 40,000 feet—390 miles on internal fuel only

As can be seen from this list, this proposed jet-powered fighter airplane would have created quite a stir in 1946, the year Lockheed promised delivery. But, unfortunately, it was not proceeded with. Its proposed powerplant, however, gained official support in June 1943 as a long-term project and thus was designated XJ37.

Since the U.S. Army Air Forces was already committed to two British turbojet engine designs—the Power Jets W.2B, to be produced by the General Electric Company in America as the J31, and the de Havilland H.1B, to be produced in America by Allis-Chalmers as the J36—it did not pursue development of the XJ37 with the same gusto. Moreover, because it was already dealing with the Bell Aircraft Corporation to produce both a twin-jet fighter (with two J31s) and a single-jet fighter (with one J36), it was not very interested in ordering Lockheed's Temporary Design Number L-133 fighter; in fact, the

Model depicting the L-133's final configuration. Lockheed

Philip A. ("Phil") Colman was a key aerodynamicist on the Temporary Design Number L-133 project. Lockheed

Willis M. Hawkins was another key
engineer on the Temporary Design

Number L-133 and other Skunk Works
projects. Lockheed

L-133 never received an official designation. Although there was hope for the XJ37, there was little reason to continue L-133 development, and as a result, it was put on the back burner.

Ultimately, too, Lockheed decided to abandon its turbojet engine development in October 1945. The XJ37, along with its design and development group, was transferred under license to the Menasco Manufacturing Company. Menasco subsequently built the prototype XJ37 under Lockheed Temporary Design Number L-4000 but did not have sufficient facilities to continue its development. Wright Aeronautical, the powerplant division of the Curtiss-Wright Corporation, assumed responsibility from Menasco for the final development work on the Lockheed XJ37. Finally, in 1950, all work on the XJ37 ended. It remains unclear exactly what happened to this advanced turbojet engine design. We can only assume that serious development problems arose before the XJ37 was perfected, or that better engines were being developed.

The designers of the proposed L-133 fighter, however, had nothing to be ashamed of. Working in concert Kelly Johnson, Philip A. ("Phil") Colman, Willis M. Hawkins, and Eugene C. ("Gene") Frost had designed a radical airframe of stainless steel with a projected performance—625 miles per hour at 50,000 feet—that was years away. Although their efforts in developing the L-133 had gone without reward, they had gained invaluable experience in their respective abilities to design advanced aircraft. By mid-1943, these same four men were working on a new jet-powered fighter, Temporary Design Number L-140. If they had not ventured forward on Temporary Design Number L-133, they would not have gained on the just-awakening world of jet aviation, which for Lockheed, in this case, proved most lucrative.

Chapter 3

F-80 Shooting Star

You don't *fly* this airplane—you just hint to it where you want to go.

—Milo Burcham

On 1 August 1945, just two weeks before the end of World War II, the U.S. Army Air Forces celebrated its thirty-eighth birthday with the public unveiling of its Lockheed P-80 Shooting Star with simultaneous showings in New York, New York, and Washington, D.C. At the time, since the war was not yet over, Lockheed Aircraft and North American Aviation were tooling up to produce thirty-five P-80s a day in five factories.

When the war ended, many military aircraft procurement and production programs were either slowed down or stopped outright. In fact, the original order for 3,500 Shooting Stars was reduced by 2,583 to 917 aircraft. This decrease was minor, however, when compared with other aircraft production cuts being made across the board following V-J Day. As one result, North American never did produce even one P-80 (F-80 after

11 June 1948, when *P* for Pursuit was changed to *F* for Fighter).

Secret Project MX-409

Earlier, on 17 May 1943, Kelly Johnson was at Eglin Army Air Field (now Eglin Air Force Base), Florida, watching a U.S. Army Air Force demonstration of the new P-38J—an improved version of Johnson's Lightning design. During this event, he was briefed on current turbojet engine developments and was told that a jet-powered airplane was flying in America. Colonel Marshall S. Roth of the U.S. Army Air Forces, at Wright Army Air Field, explained to Johnson about the flight testing on this new Bell Aircraft pursuit airplane, the P-59 Airacomet, which had proved disappointing because it was slower than the piston-powered, propeller-driven P-38 they were watching. Moreover, Colonel Roth said that the P-59 would be no match for reported German-built jet-powered aircraft.

"Kelly, you [Lockheed] wanted to build a jet for us once. Why don't you try your hand at putting a fighter airframe around the new de Havilland engine the English have promised us?" Roth asked, according to *The Shooting Star*

Story: Lockheed's P-80, a 1976 Lockheed brochure written by Tony LeVier.

"Just give me the specs on the engine," snapped back Johnson, full of his patent enthusiasm.

Johnson boarded a commercial airliner and left Florida for his return to California. En route, he scribbled fiercely on

ORIGINAL XP 80
[LULU-BELLE]

The original appearance of Lulu-Belle, the one-of-a-kind XP-80, which now resides at the National Air and Space Museum, Washington, D.C. In addition to Chief Engineer Hall Hibbard's and

Assistant Chief Engineer Kelly Johnson's signatures under Original XP-80, the signatures of the other 26 XP-80 engineers are shown. Lockheed

Chief Engineering Test Pilot Milo Burcham of Lockheed poses during P-38 Lightning flight test activities prior to his first P-80 flight test work. Unfortunately, Burcham was killed in the crash of the number three YP-80A. Lockheed

envelope backs and on magazine margins. Stepping off the plane at Lockheed Air Terminal in Burbank, he reported to President Robert Gross and Chief Engineer Hall Hibbard. It was 18 May. After taking two steps at a time up to Gross' office, where both Gross and Hibbard were waiting, Johnson said: "Wright Field wants us to submit a proposal for building a plane around an English jet engine. I've worked out some figures. I think we can promise them 180-day delivery. What do you think?"

It was more than a chance to build a new fighter airplane. It was a matter of pride. It was the culmination of wishes that dated back to 1939, when Lockheed designed what it hoped would become the first American turbojet engine, and to 1941, when Lockheed designed what it hoped would become the first American fighter powered by turbojet propulsion.

Serious discussion followed.

"O.K., Kelly, it's your baby," Gross said soberly. "We'll give you all the help we can."

But in 180 days! No airframe contractor had ever designed and built an experimental airplane in less than a year—let alone in half a year. And a jet-powered fighter was a radical departure from the contemporary piston-powered fighter. But one month after talking with Colonel Marshall Roth at Eglin, Johnson was at Wright Field with a sketch of Lockheed's

proposed Temporary Design Number L-140; twelve pages of detailed specifications, titled *Preliminary Design Investigation and Manufacturer's Brief Model Specifications*, for Secret Project MX-409; and a quotation for $524,920.

"And we'll build it in 180 days," Johnson promised General Henry H. ("Hap") Arnold, commanding general of the U.S. Army Air Forces.

"Just when would those 180 days start?" General Arnold asked cautiously.

"Whenever you say," Johnson replied. "Just as soon as we get the letter of intent."

"Well, you'd better get moving then," said General Arnold. "This is day number one. We'll have your letter of intent ready this afternoon."

On that very same day, 17 June 1943, the U.S. Army Air Forces Air Materiel Command gave the official go-ahead to the project and handed Johnson a letter contract for the production of three experimental jet-powered fighter aircraft, now designated XP-80. The letter contract, AC-40680, was for $515,018.40: the estimated cost of $495,210.00 plus a 4 percent fixed fee, versus the 6 percent fixed fee originally quoted by Lockheed. The letter contract was approved on 24 June, and a formal contract for the same amount followed on 16 October.

Earlier, in late 1942, Bell Aircraft had been asked to develop a single-engine version of its P-59 to be powered by the de Havilland Goblin turbojet engine—its Model 29, or XP-59B, under Secret Project MX-409. Owing to its lack of faith in a single-engine design, however (it was having enough trouble with its twin-engine design), Bell turned down the offer. Thus, all of Bell's preliminary design studies on its Model 29 and all the specifications and drawings on de Havilland's Goblin turbojet engine were turned over to Lockheed by the Air Materiel Command in June 1943.

By contract, the first XP-80 prototype airplane had to be completed in six months. This was a major undertaking by itself, but total secrecy was the order of the day and received the highest priority—and this secrecy called for special measures.

Total Secrecy

Total secrecy was indeed the highest priority on the new XP-80 program—period. No one, but no one, was allowed to discuss his or her work beyond the wooden walls of the makeshift experimental airplane shop constructed out of empty aircraft engine boxes and canvas. Although such discussion was temptation in the first degree, the players kept mum.

One day, just after the secret shop had been constructed, engineer Irving H. ("Irv") Culver of

The one XP-80 on the Muroc Army Air Field flight line, circa 1945. Lockheed

Lockheed was working at the phone desk. The phone rang. Culver was alone, and he had not yet been briefed on just how to answer the telephone. Being an avid fan of the *Lil' Abner* comic strips, familiar with Hairless Joe's Dogpatch Kickapoo Joy Juice brewery called the Skonk Works, where Joe made his brew out of old shoes, skunk, and other goodies, Culver answered, "Skonk Works, Culver." And Lockheed's Skunk Works was born.

To accomplish Lockheed's advanced development project in total secrecy, Kelly Johnson— assisted by William P. ("Bill") Ralston and Don Palmer—hand-picked twenty-five other engineers and 105 assembly workers. These 133 men would be responsible for the creation of America's second jet-powered airplane. Every phase of its construction would have to be highly restricted. Ralston and Palmer served as assistant project engineers, with Johnson as project engineer. Arthur M. ("Art") Vierick, chief of engineering for Lockheed's experimental department, supervised the shop group. It took ten days to construct the facility and assemble the workers.

Secret Project MX-409 was very high on the U.S. Army Air Forces' list of priorities. Giving first-class cooperation, all government-furnished equipment such as instruments, tires, guns, and so on was at Lockheed, awaiting installation, within six days after the start of the project. Lieutenant Colonel Ralph Swofford of the U.S. Army Air Forces was the original U.S. Army Air Forces XP-80 project liaison officer; he was later followed by Lieutenant Colonel Jack Carter.

A 180-day countdown calendar labeled Our Days Are Numbered was posted on the back wall of the shop, and after each 24-hour period, one day was slashed off. The countdown was slow at first, but before anyone knew it, it had considerably speeded up. Johnson kept his 10-hour day, six-day workweek schedule, however, which he had established on day number 180. No one was to work on Sundays.

As the days counted off—170, 160, 150, and downward—Johnson had to insist that his work schedule rule be obeyed. The makeshift building was drafty and cold, and the sickness rate built up to 30 percent daily—much, much too high.

"By coming back in here on Sundays, you're hurting the project," he pointed out to the group, according to *The Shooting Star Story*. "You don't get enough rest, and you get sick. The next man I catch in here on Sunday goes back to the B-17s." He never caught anyone, but between Saturday night and Monday morning, ghosts continued to get a lot of work done.

A major problem on the XP-80 manufacturing program was the

Anthony W. ("Tony") LeVier climbs into XP-80A number one for its first flight on 10 June 1944 at Muroc's North Base Area. Boarding from the aircraft's right side is noteworthy. Lockheed

XP-80A number one, Grey Ghost, during its first flight with Tony LeVier under glass. Lockheed

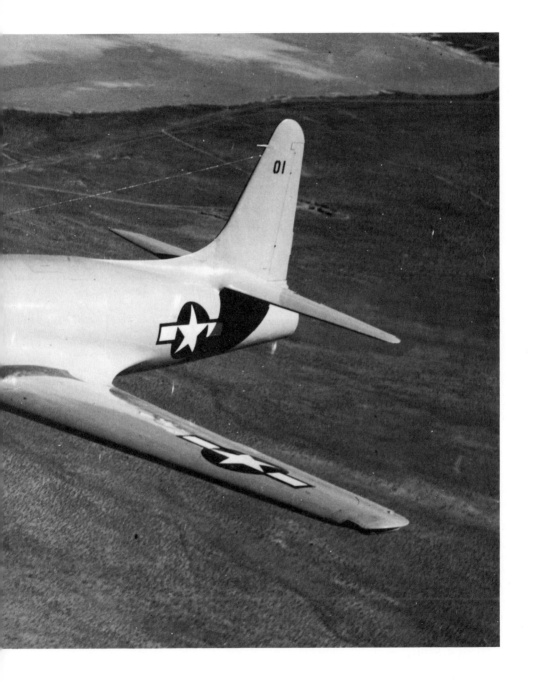

lack of the Goblin turbojet engine, which had been designed by Major Frank B. Halford of the Royal Air Force (RAF) and produced by de Havilland. Only a blueprint of the engine was in hand until seven days before the XP-80 airframe was completed. Then, as fate would have it, changes had to be made to the airframe before the engine could be fitted.

These changes, although minor, added 35 pounds to the airframe. This put the XP-80 6 pounds over the contract gross weight of 8,614 pounds. The U.S. Army Air Forces forgave this breach.

Lulu-Belle

With forty-one days still left on the countdown calendar, the XP-80, nicknamed *Lulu-Belle* by one of the mechanics, was secretly rolled out in the middle of the night and trucked to the North Base Area of Muroc Army Air Field (now Edwards Air Force Base), California. Engine run-ups began that same day; the Goblin roared to life the first time the starter button was depressed.

On day number 143, 15 November 1943, the U.S. Army Air Forces accepted the airplane as ready for flight testing. The plane was to fly the next morning, and back in Burbank, thirty-seven days remained on the countdown calendar.

Guy Bristow, de Havilland's Goblin engine expert, wanted to make sure his firm's turbojet was ready for the historic event. Late in the evening on 15 November, Bristow gave the engine a final test run. As the engine roared at full power, both of *Lulu-Belle's* engine air inlet ducts collapsed. Before he could stop the engine, pieces of duct metal were sucked into the Goblin's maw, chewed, and swallowed.

Turbojet engines are not designed to digest anything other than air and fuel. But maybe the damage would not be too serious.

Kelly Johnson broke his Sunday rule. Art Vierick, Guy Bristow, Dorsey Kammerer, and Johnson himself disassembled the engine using Bristow's tools, since it was assembled with metric nuts and bolts as used by the British.

The internal parts of the engine looked good—up to almost the end of disassembly. Then Bristow looked into the greasy, tired faces of the three men watching him. He was one of the few men on earth that knew the Goblin engine from one end to the other. "I'm frightfully sorry," he said in his British dialect. "This crack in the compressor housing . . . You'd better ask for another engine. You won't be able to fly this one," according to Tony LeVier in *The Shooting Star Story*.

Finally, after another H.1 engine was flown in from the de Havilland company in England, installed, and checked out, *Lulu-Belle* was ready to try her wings. It was the evening of 7 January 1944, and she was scheduled for an early morning liftoff the next day.

Lockheed's chief engineering test pilot, Milo Burcham, was to flight-test *Lulu-Belle*. As the airplane was prepared for flight, Johnson gave last-minute instructions to Burcham, according to *The Shooting Star Story*. "Just fly her, Milo. Find out if she's a lady or a witch. And if you have any trouble at all, bring her back. She's all yours from here. Treat her nice."

On 8 January, *Lulu-Belle* flew. After lifting off the north end of Muroc Dry Lake (now Rogers Dry Lake), Burcham initiated a climbing turn. But the wings wobbled. He nosed down and came on around to land.

Johnson hurried anxiously out to the plane and, according to *The Shooting Star Story*, asked, "What's the trouble, Milo?"

"Overcautious, maybe," Burcham answered. "She felt funny on the ailerons. Pretty touchy."

"You've got fifteen-to-one-boost and a hot ship that's naturally sensitive; maybe you were overcontrolling," Johnson said.

"Could be," Burcham agreed.

Kelly Johnson congratulates Tony LeVier after his successful first flight in the first XP-80A. Lockheed

Burcham restarted the engine and took off again. This time, *Lulu-Belle* flew straight and true. Burcham made one low pass across the lake bed and zoomed up and out of sight. Then the show began.

Accustomed to the controls, Burcham dropped down from high altitude so fast that no one knew he was coming until he passed overhead, and the roar of the engine's exhaust hit the onlookers. According to *The Shooting Star Story*, Johnson later recalled: "It was a blast of sound that surrounded us without seeming to originate anywhere. It was a new

sensation then." Burcham came back across the field doing full aileron rolls, the XP-80 snapping around and around, while below, men who had worked 10-hour days, six days a week, and sneaked back to their job on Sundays, stood with tears in their eyes.

Burcham later said, "You don't *fly* this airplane; you just hint to it where you want to go."

Grey Ghost and *Silver Ghost*
Lulu-Belle had proved she was a lady—a fast lady, hitting 502 miles per hour at sea level—everything Lockheed, and the U.S. Army Air Forces, had dreamed of.

This right-side profile of XP-80A number one illustrates the type's simple and clean design. Lockheed

U.S. Army Air Forces officers had watched her perform, and they were both surprised and delighted. They of course wanted more jets— soon.

Allis-Chalmers' J36 Goblin engines, however, would not be available in quantity anytime soon. But General Electric was speeding up production on a revised British turbojet engine design, General Electric Model I-40, designated J33. The engine was bigger and heavier and produced more thrust —up to 4,000 pounds. Thus, it required an almost new airframe. Could Lockheed build it?

"Can do," said Johnson, according to *The Shooting Star Story*, and this time his talented group brewed up the first of two prototypes in 132 days and flew it on the 138th day.

Test pilot Anthony W. ("Tony") LeVier of Lockheed flew it for the first time on 10 June 1944 off the main runway at Muroc Army Air Field. Designated XP-80A because of its differences from the original XP-80, and called the *Grey Ghost* because of its grey paint scheme, this airplane with its General Electric J33 engine was even more sensational.

Lockheed completed the second XP-80A in a natural aluminum alloy finish, and it was therefore nicknamed the *Silver Ghost*. Likewise powered by a single J33-GE-11 engine, it was first flown by Tony LeVier on 1 August 1944 at Muroc Army Air Field; this plane

survived flight test activities and became an engine testbed for the XF-90 penetration fighter program and an air vehicle for other tests such as the incorporation of externally mounted fuel tanks for the Shooting Star program. XP-80A number one, however, was not so fortunate.

On 20 March 1945, while *Grey Ghost* was leveling off at 11,000 feet after a dive from 15,000 feet to end a speed run, a turbine wheel in its engine failed. The disintegration of that wheel sliced off the plane's entire tail group. At 11,000 feet and a speed of 575 miles per hour, and without any warning whatsoever, the nose of the plane dropped downward. It then swerved violently to the left, and the plane began to tumble out of control. Tony LeVier pulled the canopy release, and when the plane became inverted, he was catapulted out of the cockpit at an altitude of about 4,000 feet. Fearing the plane would strike him, LeVier rolled into a ball and closed his eyes.

Since the plane did not hit him, he opted to straighten out and open his eyes for his parachute landing. The plane was on an even keel with him and falling at the same rate. LeVier's small-diameter parachute caused him to fall too fast and made his body oscillate too much. Thus, he impacted the ground too hard to walk away under his own power. Suffering from a severe back injury, for which he was forced to wear a steel back brace during his recovery, he spent four months in a hospital. But as soon as his doctor signed his release, he was back in the saddle of an early production P-80A—and fighting for larger-diameter chutes for improved pilot safety.

Meanwhile, the U.S. Army Air Forces issued Lockheed an initial contract for thirteen service test YP-80A aircraft. This was soon followed by an order for 3,500 production P-80s for the war effort. But (as mentioned earlier) that order was reduced after V-J Day.

Nonetheless, the legacy of the Shooting Star, as the type was officially named—indeed, that of Lockheed's Skunk Works and all it has created since—had been born.

Unfortunately, no record exists of the names of the Skunk Works' first group of assembly workers. But here are the names of the twenty-eight original Skunk Works engineers:

H. L. Benson
W. L. Bison
Dick Boehme
L. J. Bohacek
H. R. Bojens
A. Bradley
G. F. Brown
Irving H. Culver
H. C. Danielson
Edward Fife
G. W. Gossett
Hall L. Hibbard
D. C. Hill
R. L. Holland
Clarence L. Johnson
J. A. Johnson

Left-side profile of XP-80A number two, Silver Ghost, *which became an engine testbed for the afterburning Westing-house YJ34-WE-15 turbojet engine in support of the XF-90 penetration fighter program, circa 1950. Lockheed*

J. F. Kerr
R. L. Kirkham
V. D. Moss
P. W. McLane
Don Palmer
William P. Ralston
Henry F. Rempt
W. M. Stearman
Charles C. Sowle
Joe Szep
Arthur M. Vierick
A. J. York

The Lockheed F-80 Shooting Star holds the distinction of being America's, and the U.S. Air Force's, first operational jet-powered fighter airplane. This prominence, however, could not have come about if not for the minor wartime miracle that Kelly Johnson—and his original team of Skunk Works players—pulled off in 1943. Moreover, the F-80 formed the matrix that molded several major spin-off aircraft, which included the T-33 jet trainer, F-94 Starfire, and T-1 SeaStar.

XP-80 Specifications

Type	Single-seat, single-engine experimental day fighter
Wingspan	37 feet
Wing area	240 square feet
Length	32 feet, 10 inches
Height	10 feet, 3 inches
Empty weight	6,287 pounds
Maximum weight	8,916 pounds
Maximum speed	502 miles per hour at 20,480 feet (attained)
Service ceiling	41,000 feet
Rate of climb	3,000 feet per minute
Maximum range	Unknown
Armament	6 .50 caliber machine guns; 1,200 rounds of ammunition
Powerplant	1 nonafterburning de Havilland Halford H.1B Goblin turbojet engine

XP-80A Specifications

Type	Single-seat, single-engine experimental day fighter
Wingspan	39 feet
Wing area	237.6 square feet
Length	34 feet, 6 inches
Height	11 feet, 4 inches
Empty weight	7,225 pounds
Maximum weight	13,780 pounds
Maximum speed	553 miles per hour at 5,700 feet
Service ceiling	48,500 feet
Rate of climb	3,000 feet per minute

Maximum range	1,200 miles
Armament	6 .50 caliber machine guns; 1,200 rounds of ammunition
Powerplant	1 nonafterburning General Electric J33-GE-11 (Model I-40) turbojet engine; XP-80A number 2 was reengined with an afterburning Westinghouse J34-WE-15 in support of the XF-90 penetration fighter program

XP-80 and XP-80A Production

Model Number	Designation	Serial Number	Comments
TDN L-140	XP-80-00-LO	44-83020	Displayed at the National Air and Space Museum, Washington, D.C.
TDN L-141	XP-80A-00-LO	44-83021	Lost in crash on 20 March 1945
TDN L-141	XP-80A-00-LO	44-83022	Engine testbed for the J34-WE-15 turbojet engine in the XF-90 program; its final disposition is unknown

Chapter 4

T-33 T-Bird and T-1A SeaStar

The government needs a jet trainer. Right now they don't want it but they're going to get it, and I think they will like it.

—Kelly Johnson

Since 1,732 P-80 and F-80 Shooting Stars were built by Lockheed before more advanced jet-powered fighter types appeared, the company's F-80 program was undoubtedly a complete success. In early 1945, however, while still undergoing developmental flight tests and evaluations, an unacceptable number of them had crashed. One crash took the life of America's leading World War II ace, Major Richard I. Bong of the United States Army Air Forces, who was credited with forty confirmed kills. Another crash took the life of Chief Engineering Test Pilot Milo Burcham of Lockheed. Primarily, these crashes and others were attributed to pilot errors. Jet-powered aircraft were still very new, and most pilots couldn't just jump out of piston-powered, propeller-driven aircraft and then simply jump into jet-powered

aircraft. It didn't, and doesn't, work that way.

In this light, Mac V. F. Short, Lockheed vice-president in charge of military relations, foresaw the need for a two-seat version of the P-80 for dedicated jet pilot training and transition. In late 1945, Short approached Lockheed management with his prudent concern. Lockheed, however, was still trying to prove its P-80 was airworthy and safe in hope of continued sales in a postwar atmosphere. Moreover, since the type was often crashing, Lockheed thought it wasn't an appropriate time to offer another version of it to potential users. It simply didn't want to upset the apple cart. Although Short's idea was well received in-house, Lockheed management placed it in limbo— at least, for the time being. In early 1947, however, after the F-80 had proved to be a reliable jet fighter,

The number three TP-80C (later re-designated TF-80C and T-33A) production T-Bird shows its lengthened fuselage and cockpit canopy in its raised position. Note the absence of any .50 caliber machine gun nose ports; all production T-33As had at least two gun ports. Lockheed

and because additional orders for it were in hand, Lockheed decided to move forward with Short's plan to provide America with its first dedicated jet-powered trainer airplane.

T-33 T-Bird

To begin, using in-house monies, Lockheed management directed the Skunk Works to design a two-seat derivative of the Shooting Star for possible sales to both the U.S. Air Force and U.S. Navy—to replace their piston-powered, propeller-driven, North American–built trainers, the T-6 and SNJ respectively. Since neither service had a jet-powered trainer, and because neither service required such an aircraft, Lockheed's Skunk Works clamped a tight lid on the project in its attempt to gain a head start on its competition. Ultimately, in a big way, this ploy worked, and Lockheed went on to produce 5,691 examples for the U.S. Air Force, U.S. Navy, and U.S. Marine Corps.

It all began in May 1947 when Skunk Works leader Hall Hibbard appointed Don Palmer to serve as head engineer on what became Lockheed Model 580. In August 1947, just three short months later, Palmer's Model 580 design was ready for in-house scrutiny. To Palmer and his team's delight, it was immediately accepted and approved by Lockheed management.

To design Lockheed Model 580, based on the C-model of the Shooting Star, Palmer and his teammates engineered the changes as follows:

• Removed four of the six .50 caliber machine guns and their linked equipment to decrease weight and to increase already available room for the addition of a second cockpit.

• Redesigned the fuselage to provide a second cockpit for the instructor pilot behind the student pilot by (1) inserting a plug 12 inches long aft of the wing, (2) inserting a 38.6 inch plug ahead of the wing, and (3) reducing the fuselage fuel capacity from 207 gallons to 95 gallons. Larger-capacity nylon fuel cells were then placed in the wings, replacing the F-80C's self-sealing tanks, to raise the total internal fuel capacity to 353 gallons—that is, 72 fewer gallons than the F-80C carried; provision was made for two 230 gallons centerline wing tip tanks.

• Installed dual emergency ejection seats under a lengthy one-piece cockpit canopy—the longest at the time—that raised manually in an emergency or electrically in normal operation. For the instructor pilot's forward visibility over student pilots, the aft cockpit floor was raised.

In keeping two .50 caliber machine guns and leaving provision for underwing stores a la the F-80C, the Model 580 could double as either a pilot trainer or a combat trainer—a major sales point. The time had come to propose the design, and in August 1947, Lockheed took its unsolicited Model 580 proposal to U.S. Air Force Air Materiel Command at Wright Field. It was well received.

As a result, the U.S. Air Force authorized Lockheed to remove a single P-80C airframe from its Burbank assembly line for conversion into a tandem-seat trainer prototype. Since the P-80C was already proved, and in production, the trainer prototype did not receive the status quo *X* (experimental) or *Y* (service test) prefix. It was simply designated TP-80C, meaning it was a pursuit trainer aircraft based on the C-model of the P-80 Shooting Star. After 11 June 1948, however—after *P* for Pursuit gave way to *F* for Fighter—the TP-80C was redesignated TF-80C.

Modification of the single P-80C airframe, U.S. Air Force serial number 48-356, into the TP-80C went forward as planned and without any major problems. Then, on 22 March 1948, Chief Engineering Test Pilot Tony LeVier of Lockheed made its successful first flight out of Van Nuys Airport, California. It was found to handle and perform much like the P-80C, and it even went faster, with comparable engine throttle settings.

On 7 April 1948, a U.S. Air Force contract was approved for twenty TP-80C aircraft; eight more were ordered twenty days later, and 128 more on 10 November. America's first jet-powered trainer airplane was in production. Mac Short's vision had been realized.

Powered by a nonafterburning Allison J33-A-23 turbojet engine of

Having made its first flight, Tony LeVier poses with a T-33A on Lockheed's Burbank flight line circa 1948. At one time, the T-33 was the most widely flown jet airplane in the world. Ten years after it was introduced, 90 percent of all the free world's jet pilots were trained in this popular two-place schoolship—flown by the U.S. Air Force, U.S. Navy, and U.S. Marine Corps as the T-33A or -33B, and by 23 friendly powers. Lockheed

4,600 pounds thrust, the first production TF-80C was accepted by the U.S. Air Force on 31 August 1948—just one year after Lockheed had offered its Model 580 design to the U.S. Air Force as an unsolicited proposal.

Like the U.S. Air Force, the U.S. Navy was procuring jet-powered fighters. Whereas the U.S. Air Force was operating its land-based Shooting Stars, Thunderjets, and Sabres, the U.S. Navy was operating its carrier-based Furys, Phantoms, and Panthers. Therefore, it also required jet-

powered trainers. In 1949, under existing U.S. Air Force contracts, it initiated procurement of Lockheed TO-2s (TF-80Cs navalized by strengthening the airframe and landing gear and adding a tailhook). These aircraft, as well as follow-on TV-2s (redesignated TO-2s), were built alongside U.S. Air Force TF-80Cs (redesignated T-33As on 5 May 1949); U.S. Navy and U.S. Marine Corps TV-2s were redesignated T-33Bs in 1962.

All in all, Lockheed produced 4,992 T-33As for the U.S. Air Force and another 699 T-33Bs for the

As a 600 mile per hour development of the F-80 Shooting Star, the T-33 became the world standard for higher education for future jet fighter pilots.

The T-Bird's planform is clearly shown here as a T-33A banks off toward the left, while the T-33A in the foreground shows off its profile in flight. Lockheed

U.S. Navy and U.S. Marine Corps, for a total of 5,691 T-Bird aircraft, as the type was nicknamed—3,959 more than the company's total production run of F-80 Shooting Stars, from which the T-33As and T-33Bs evolved. Moreover, Canada (Canadair) and Japan (Kawasaki) produced another 866 T-Birds under license: respectively, 656 and 210. All total, 6,557 T-Birds were built.

At this point, with clever Skunk Works engineering, out of a single basic design of an experimental fighter plane dubbed *Lulu-Belle* came 8,289 F-80 Shooting Stars and T-33 T-Birds. But the airframe that produced all these F-80s and T-33s wasn't through yet, as it spawned two more major aircraft programs for Lockheed: the T-1A SeaStar (discussed in the next section of this chapter) and the F-94 Starfire (discussed in the following chapter).

T-1A SeaStar

In October 1952, again using in-house monies, Lockheed set out to develop an improved carrier-based jet trainer airplane for the U.S. Navy.

Using the T-33 as the base, a number of designs were drawn up by Kelly Johnson and his teammates in the Skunk Works' preliminary design department. They settled on Temporary Design Number L-245, believing it would satisfy the U.S. Navy at home and,

possibly, foreign users abroad. The design, closely resembling that of the T-33 but very different in many ways, was frozen in early 1953. It featured, in part, the following:

● Incorporation of leading edge slats on the wings, a larger-area tail group with horizontal and vertical stabilizers, and a boundary layer control system to improve the aircraft's low-speed handling characteristics

● Installation of a larger cockpit canopy, and raising of the aft cockpit floor 6 inches to improve greatly the forward vision of instructor pilots

● Installation of an arresting hook for carrier landings, and incorporation of the nonafterburning Allison J33-A-16A turbojet engine with 5,200 pounds of thrust

Lockheed opted to build a demonstrator airplane with its own funds. To do this, it bought back an uncompleted U.S. Air Force T-33A airframe, U.S. Air Force serial number 52-9255, and moved ahead with the construction of Temporary Design Number L-245. Unofficially known as the T-33B (the next model of the T-33, before the U.S. Navy's TV-2 was redesignated T-33B) and named the Lockheed trainer, the company-owned prototype, assigned civil registration number N125D, was completed and rolled out on 30 November 1953.

On 16 December 1953, under the capable guidance of Tony

LeVier, the Lockheed trainer made its first flight out of the Lockheed Air Terminal at Burbank. It was a good first trip, but subsequent flights demonstrated that aerodynamic refinements were in order.

Flight testing showed that the aircraft's raised cockpit canopy restricted the airflow around the vertical stabilizer. To correct this, Lockheed added a larger dorsal fairing between the aft cockpit area and the forward area of the vertical fin. Also, to reduce excessive

boattail drag, the exterior of the turbojet engine's tailpipe was redesigned. With these changes, the airplane proved to be stable about all three axes—pitch, roll, and yaw—and a pleasure to fly.

Lockheed demonstrated its advanced trainer to the U.S. Air Force and U.S. Navy. The U.S. Air Force, satisfied with its T-33A, passed on the plane. The U.S. Navy, wanting a dedicated carrier-based jet trainer, ordered an initial batch of eight aircraft. Temporary Design Number L-245 was then

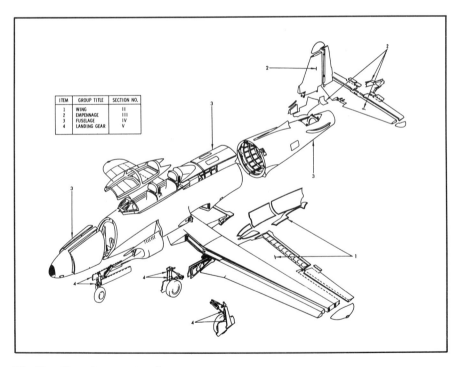

ITEM	GROUP TITLE	SECTION NO.
1	WING	II
2	EMPENNAGE	III
3	FUSELAGE	IV
4	LANDING GEAR	V

The T-33A's major structural groups, as assembled on the production line. U.S. Air Force

designated Model 1080 by Lockheed and T2V-1 by the U.S. Navy. Now powered by nonafterburning Allison-built J33-A-24 or -24A turbojet engines with 6,100 pounds of thrust, the T2V-1

(redesignated the T-1A on 18 September 1962) was given the official name SeaStar. In all, the U.S. Navy ordered 149 production SeaStars before buying unarmed

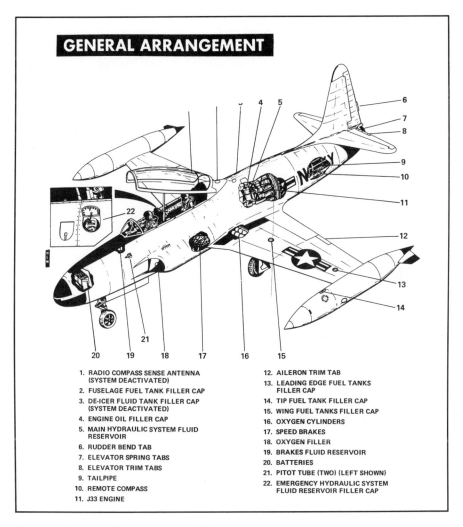

GENERAL ARRANGEMENT

1. RADIO COMPASS SENSE ANTENNA (SYSTEM DEACTIVATED)
2. FUSELAGE FUEL TANK FILLER CAP
3. DE-ICER FLUID TANK FILLER CAP (SYSTEM DEACTIVATED)
4. ENGINE OIL FILLER CAP
5. MAIN HYDRAULIC SYSTEM FLUID RESERVOIR
6. RUDDER BEND TAB
7. ELEVATOR SPRING TABS
8. ELEVATOR TRIM TABS
9. TAILPIPE
10. REMOTE COMPASS
11. J33 ENGINE

12. AILERON TRIM TAB
13. LEADING EDGE FUEL TANKS FILLER CAP
14. TIP FUEL TANK FILLER CAP
15. WING FUEL TANKS FILLER CAP
16. OXYGEN CYLINDERS
17. SPEED BRAKES
18. OXYGEN FILLER
19. BRAKES FLUID RESERVOIR
20. BATTERIES
21. PITOT TUBE (TWO) (LEFT SHOWN)
22. EMERGENCY HYDRAULIC SYSTEM FLUID RESERVOIR FILLER CAP

The T-33B's general arrangement. U.S. Navy

A T-33B (formerly designated TO-1 and TV-2) trainer for the U.S. Navy and U.S. Marine Corps. As still another version of the basic F-80 airframe, this two-place jet trainer was capable of 600 mile per hour speed. Lockheed

The first production T-1A (formerly T2V-1) SeaStar during its first flight. Note the extended speed brakes. Lockheed

North American T-2 Buckeyes and armed Grumman TF-9Js.

Although this airplane production program was not quite as successful as earlier programs, it proved how adaptive a sound airframe design can be. Even earlier, before the advent of the T-1A SeaStar, this amazing airframe had given birth to still another winner: the F-94 Starfire.

T-33A Specifications

Type	Tandem-seat, single-engine pilot trainer and transition aircraft
Wingspan	38 feet, 10.5 inches
Wing area	234.8 square feet
Length	37 feet, 9 inches
Height	11 feet, 8 inches
Empty weight	8,365 pounds
Maximum weight	15,061 pounds
Maximum speed	600 miles per hour
Service ceiling	48,000 feet
Rate of climb	4,870 feet per minute
Maximum range	1,275 miles
Armament	2 .50 caliber machine guns (optional)
Powerplant	1 nonafterburning Allison J33-A-35 turbojet engine

Note: Lockheed built 5,691 T-33s, Canadair built 656 T-33s, and Kawasaki built 210 T-33s, for a total of 6,557 T-Birds produced; 150 T-1A SeaStars were also built.

Chapter 5

F-94 Starfire

KISS ... Keep It Simple, Stupid.

—Kelly Johnson; motto of the Skunk Works.

If a fighter plane proves itself and demonstrates a potential for continued growth, as the Shooting Star did, its user and other possible users will take note for future reference. When a new requirement emerges—one that could be filled by an existing airframe and powerplant combination—the user will refer back to its winning combinations. In this case, the user was the U.S. Air Force, and the Allison J33-powered F-80 was the winning combination. The new requirement was for an interim, *limited*, all-weather fighter capable of nighttime operations, to be used until the Northrop F-89 Scorpion entered service.

As the year 1948 began, Lockheed was building two versions of its successful Shooting Star daytime-only fighter: the P-80C for the U.S. Air Force and the TO-1, a version of the P-80C, for the U.S. Marine Corps. From the Shooting Star airframe too,

Lockheed was gearing up to produce the tandem-seat TP-80C for the U.S. Air Force, its Air Training Command in particular. The U.S. Air Force, needing a two-seater to fill its temporary night fighter requirement, referred back to the notes it had taken on Lockheed's Shooting Star.

On 23 March 1948, the day after the first flight of the prototype TP-80C the U.S. Air Force approached Lockheed management with a welcome proposition that would ultimately create still another tandem-seat version of the popular Shooting Star, the Starfire series of F-94s.

At the time, both Curtiss and Northrop were developing tandem-seat, all-weather fighter prototypes. Although the Curtiss XF-87 Blackhawk beat the Northrop XF-89 Scorpion into the air by some five months (flying on 5 March 1948 versus 16 August 1948), the U.S. Air Force favored the latter. In fact, the Blackhawk's demise loomed large on the horizon because it was too large and too heavy. Its total 12,000 pounds of thrust was never going to be able to propel the aircraft, weighing 50,000 pounds, to 550 miles per hour, as the U.S. Air Force required.

The U.S. Air Force instead had a great deal of faith in Northrop's F-89 and was determined to proceed with its development. It

YF-94 number one was created from TF-80C (later T-33A) number one. New auxiliary Fletcher fuel tanks mounted on the wing tip centerline had just been installed for flight test evaluation. Lockheed

YF-94 number one during its first flight with pilot Tony LeVier and flight test engineer Glen Fulkerson under glass. Note the installation of original under-wing-mounted drop-type fuel tanks. Lockheed

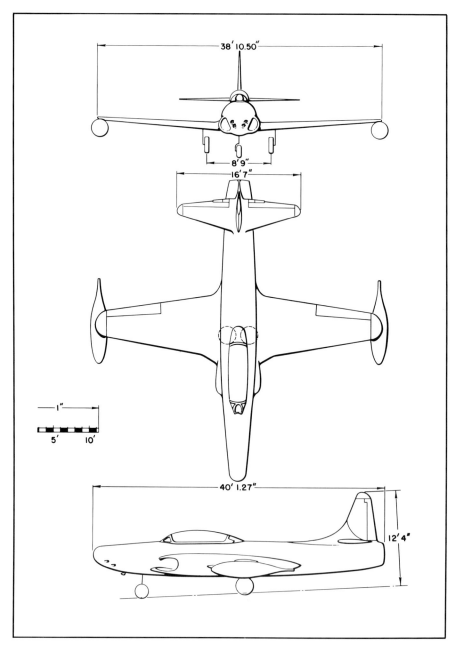

Three-view drawing of the F-94A.
Lockheed

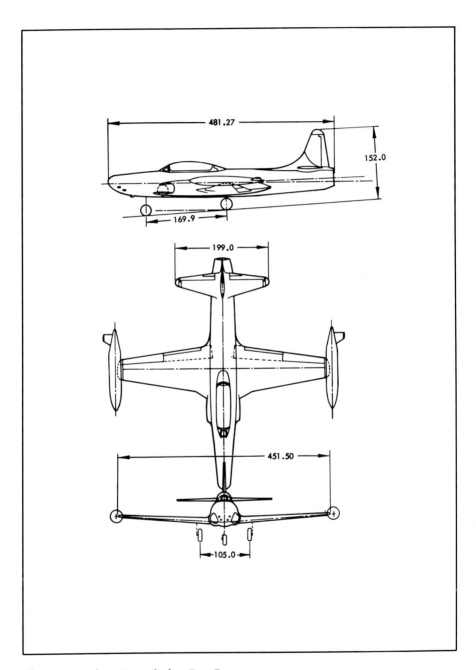

Three-view drawing of the F-94B.
Lockheed

became apparent, however, that its development was slowing down rather than speeding up. Nevertheless, it was superior to the Curtiss F-87, and it was going to be produced. With this knowledge, the U.S. Air Force created its interim, limited, all-weather nighttime fighter requirement. Owing to its knowledge of the successful F-80 program, it went to Lockheed for assistance. Making another prudent move, it also went to Douglas Aircraft. Douglas had a new prototype night fighter flying for the U.S. Navy that might also fit the bill, the XF3D-1 Skyknight,

which had made its first flight on 23 March 1948, the same day the U.S. Air Force began discussing a modified TP-80C with Lockheed.

With most of its focus on the TP-80C airframe and powerplant combination, the U.S. Air Force asked Lockheed if it could and would develop an interim all-weather fighter from it, listing, in part, the following requirements:
● Incorporation of the advanced Hughes Aircraft E-1 electronic fire control system, comprising the AN/APG-33 search-type ranging radar set, and the improved A-1C gun sight

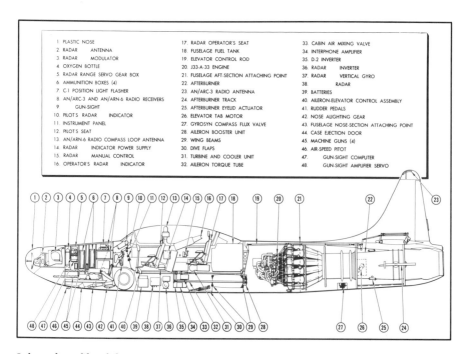

1. PLASTIC NOSE	17. RADAR OPERATOR'S SEAT	33. CABIN AIR MIXING VALVE
2. RADAR ANTENNA	18. FUSELAGE FUEL TANK	34. INTERPHONE AMPLIFIER
3. RADAR MODULATOR	19. ELEVATOR CONTROL ROD	35. D-2 INVERTER
4. OXYGEN BOTTLE	20. J33-A-33 ENGINE	36. RADAR INVERTER
5. RADAR RANGE SERVO GEAR BOX	21. FUSELAGE AFT-SECTION ATTACHING POINT	37. RADAR VERTICAL GYRO
6. AMMUNITION BOXES (4)	22. AFTERBURNER	38. RADAR
7. C-1 POSITION LIGHT FLASHER	23. AN/ARC-3 RADIO ANTENNA	39. BATTERIES
8. AN/ARC-3 AND AN/ARN-6 RADIO RECEIVERS	24. AFTERBURNER TRACK	40. AILERON-ELEVATOR CONTROL ASSEMBLY
9. GUN-SIGHT	25. AFTERBURNER EYELID ACTUATOR	41. RUDDER PEDALS
10. PILOT'S RADAR INDICATOR	26. ELEVATOR TAB MOTOR	42. NOSE ALIGHTING GEAR
11. INSTRUMENT PANEL	27. GYROSYN COMPASS FLUX VALVE	43. FUSELAGE NOSE-SECTION ATTACHING POINT
12. PILOT'S SEAT	28. AILERON BOOSTER UNIT	44. CASE EJECTION DOOR
13. AN/ARN-6 RADIO COMPASS LOOP ANTENNA	29. WING BEAMS	45. MACHINE GUNS (4)
14. RADAR INDICATOR POWER SUPPLY	30. DIVE FLAPS	46. AIR-SPEED PITOT
15. RADAR MANUAL CONTROL	31. TURBINE AND COOLER UNIT	47. GUN-SIGHT COMPUTER
16. OPERATOR'S RADAR INDICATOR	32. AILERON TORQUE TUBE	48. GUN-SIGHT AMPLIFIER SERVO

Inboard profile of the F-94A and -94B.
Lockheed

Tony LeVier inspects the new
sweptback horizontal tail on the first
YF-94C (formerly YF-97A). Lockheed

A fine study of YF-94C number one on
Rogers Dry Lake, Edwards Air Force
Base. Lockheed

The first flight of YF-94C-1 with pilot
Tony LeVier and engineer Glen Fulkerson. Lockheed

- Accommodation for a radar operator in the aft cockpit
- Installation of a single, afterburning, centrifugal-flow J33-A-33 turbojet engine with 4,400 pounds of military thrust and 6,000 pounds of afterburning thrust
- Maximum speed of at least 550 miles per hour
- Installation of basic armament consisting of four .50 caliber machine guns with 300 rounds of ammunition each
- Provision for two wing tip–mounted 165 gallon auxiliary drop-type fuel tanks
- Delivery date for first production article to be no later than December 1949, or in twenty-one months

The answer the U.S. Air Force got from Lockheed management was a quick "Yes!" Thus, Lockheed was awarded a contract to modify a pair of TP-80C airframes into prototype interim, all-weather night fighters. The new airplane was designated F-94, and keeping with the Lockheed tradition of naming its aircraft after heavenly bodies, it was named Starfire.

Kelly Johnson was still the Skunk Works' assistant chief engineer and chief research engineer. He entrusted the development of Model 780, the YF-94, to a relative newcomer: Rus Daniell, who had already demonstrated his talent as an aeronautical engineer and had solid goals for his future. Daniell

formed a development team and went to work.

The Hughes E-1 electronic fire control system comprised the AN/APG-33 radar set and a network of frames filled with vacuum tubes. Although Hughes had engineered the system to fit within the narrow confines of a fighter plane's nose, it was quite lengthy. Therefore, the prototype YF-94 would have a longer nose section than either its F-80 or TF-80 counterpart aircraft.

To create the first of two YF-94 prototypes in the shortest possible time, Lockheed's Skunk Works was authorized to modify the first TF-80C prototype. The second YF-94 prototype, with all-up systems, was to be made from a TF-80C off the production line.

Working on the first TF-80C prototype airframe, Skunk Works shop technicians installed a radar operator's station within its rear cockpit; used a nonafterburning J33-A-23 engine (the J33-A-33 with afterburner was not yet ready); incorporated the Hughes E-1 electronic fire control system; installed four M3 .50 caliber machine guns—two on either side of the lower nose area—with their associated ammunition cans, link belt feeds, and so on; reduced internal fuel volume by 30 gallons to 318 gallons total; made provisions for two 165 gallon tanks under the wing tips; and enlarged the tail surfaces. The airplane was completed ahead of schedule in

March 1949, and after a series of low- and medium-speed taxi tests at the Van Nuys Airport, it was ready for its first flight.

On 16 April 1949, Chief Test Pilot Tony LeVier took off on the prototype YF-94's first flight. Glen Fulkerson, a highly qualified flight test engineer who became flight test project engineer on the F-94 program, was in the back cockpit. He would monitor the new instrumentation for U.S. Air Force radar operators. It was a successful test hop without any problems, but also without the afterburning J33 engine.

Lockheed's development effort for the F-94 had moved forward much like that for the aircraft's Starfire namesake. It had moved too fast, though, for Allison to deliver its specified J33-A-33, Model 400-D9, jet engine, which was to provide an additional 1,400 pounds of thrust with afterburning. Since the prototype YF-94 weighed 1 ton more than the TF-80C prototype from where it had come, acquisition of the more powerful J33 was paramount.

On 10 November 1948, some five months before the YF-94 took wing, the U.S. Air Force had

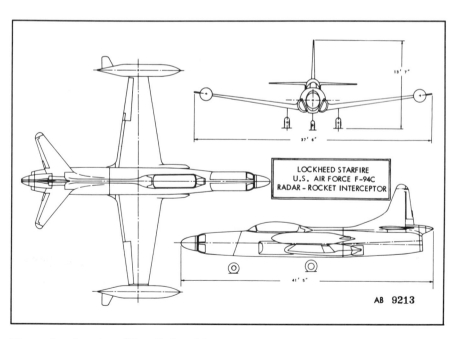

Three-view drawing of F-94C, the ulti-mate Starfire. Lockheed

ordered 110 production F-94As. Development problems on the Northrop F-89 Scorpion program, which had also beat out Douglas' F3D Skyknight, were mounting. This dilemma forced the U.S. Air Force to procure the F-94 sight unseen, performance unproved. But, as it turned out, it did not purchase a lemon.

The first flight of the second YF-94 prototype number two, with all-up systems, once again with LeVier and Fulkerson under glass, came about some four months after the first flight, on 10 August 1949.

It was judged a successful test hop, and the airplane sported the afterburning J33-A-33 engine.

Dictated by the U.S. Air Force and promised by Lockheed, the first production F-94A was delivered to and accepted by the U.S. Air Force on 10 December 1949. Thus, in early 1950, fully missionized F-94A Starfires began rolling out of Lockheed's Burbank assembly plant, which was now producing F-80C, TO-1, TF-80C, and F-94A aircraft on parallel assembly lines. By the beginning of May 1950, F-94As were being

Exploded drawing of major F-94C components. Lockheed

delivered to two user squadrons: the 317th and 319th Fighter All Weather Squadrons of the 325th Fighter Group, based respectively at McChord Air Force Base, Washington, and Moses Lake Air Force Base, Washington. The U.S. Air Force now had its interim all-weather fighter. It was a good thing it did, because the F-89 was not yet being produced.

Lockheed proposed an advanced version of the F-94A, which it *unofficially* designated YF-94B. It was advanced enough to warrant a fair amount of redesign. The U.S. Air Force was not ready for Lockheed's offering and rejected it. But it was ready for an improved version of the F-94A, which it *officially* designated YF-94B.

To create the one-of-a-kind YF-94B service test airplane, Lockheed was authorized to modify the nineteenth production F-94A block number five airframe while it was still on the Starfire production line. It became Model 780-76-12 and featured the following improvements:

• Incorporation of Sperry Zero-Reader gyroscopic instruments— comprising the AN/ARN-12

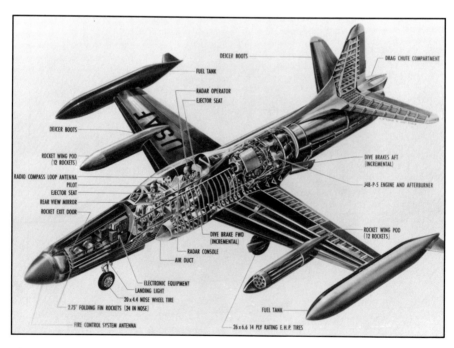

Phantom view of F-94C Starfire.
Lockheed

marker beacon receiver, the AN/ARN-5B glide path receiver, and the RC-105D localizer receiver—which provided for easier landings in foul weather

• Employment of a high-volume oxygen system and an improved cockpit pressurization system

• Addition of a 1,500 pounds per square inch hydraulic system, replacing the F-94A's 1,000 pounds per square inch system

• Incorporation of windshield defogging and antiicing equipment and provision for more head room in the aft cockpit for the radar operator

• Incorporation of the new 230 gallon Fletcher-type auxiliary fuel tanks, now mounted centrally on the wing tips, which were later retrofitted on F-94As

The YF-94B retained the Hughes E-1 electronic fire control system and AN/APG-33 radar set, and the F-94A's J33-A-33 engine and machine gun armament. The one YF-94B made its first flight on 29 September 1950 with Tony LeVier piloting, and the type was ordered into production.

Earlier, during the year 1949, two important advancements came about: first, the advent of the advanced Hughes E-5 electronic fire control system, comprising the AN/APG-40 radar set and AN/APG-84 computer, and second, the advent of the Pratt & Whitney Model JT7 afterburning J48 turbojet engine. These two new developments led to the reoffering

of Lockheed Temporary Design Number L-188, which Lockheed had proposed earlier as the *unofficial* YF-94B version, to the U.S. Air Force. The U.S. Air Force still was not interested, and therefore Lockheed took its own initiative to develop the type with its own funds within its Skunk Works. The reason for this action was that its newly proposed version of the Starfire would more than equal the performance and the firepower of the upcoming all-weather, all-rocket-armed interceptor airplane, the D-model of the Northrop F-89.

With U.S. Air Force authorization, Lockheed leased back the 151st production F-94B, U.S. Air Force serial number 50-955, for modification into an advanced all-weather, all-rocket-armed interceptor plane, Model 880. It would feature the Hughes E-5 electronic fire control system, Hughes AN/APG-40 radar set, J48 turbojet engine, and aerodynamic improvements.

The centrifugal-flow J48 engine—essentially a Rolls-Royce Tay to be produced in the United States by Pratt & Whitney—was slightly larger and heavier than the General Electric J33 engine but offered 2,300 pounds more thrust with afterburning.

To create the service test Model 880, Lockheed redesigned the F-94B's nose section to accommodate (1) the Hughes E-5 fire control system, (2) the Hughes

*An early production F-94C prior to the
incorporation of midwing rocket pods.*
Lockheed

AN/APG-40 radar set, (3) the AN/APA-84 computer, and (4) twenty-four Aeromite Mighty Mouse 2.75 inch diameter folding-fin aircraft rockets. It was a novel enough design that the U.S. Air Force finally recognized Lockheed's effort and, as a result, ordered a fully optimized service test example designated YF-97A. This example was to complement the privately funded one Lockheed had begun work on. The airplane got a new designation because it was quite different from either the F-94A or F-94B aircraft. But the dissimilarity proved temporary, and the airplane was later redesignated YF-94C.

During redesign, Advanced Development Projects

aerodynamicists thinned the wings and tail group surfaces to increase the aircraft's maximum Mach number to 0.8, increased the area of the tail group surfaces for improved high-speed stability, and made the front and rear cockpits more user friendly for both the pilot and the radar operator. In addition, the horizontal tail planes were given sweepback, and the fuselage-mounted speed brake doors were moved to the aft fuselage section, which was a completely redesigned unit (the speed brakes had been located nearer to the midfuselage area on the F-94A and -94B aircraft, ventrally, under the aft cockpit). But the biggest improvement other than the robotlike avionics was the

F-94B, U.S. Air Force serial number 51-5501, served as the aerodynamic prototype for the proposed F-94D. The aircraft is shown after M61 Vulcan cannon installation in support of Weapon System 303A, the F-104, since XF-104 number two, the armament test-bed, had crashed. Lockheed

Rus Daniell was a Skunk Works aero-dynamicist on the Starfire project.
Lockheed

employment of the Pratt & Whitney J48-PW-5 turbojet engine with 8,750 pounds of afterburning thrust.

On 19 January 1950, after the aircraft was trucked to Edwards Air Force Base and customary preflight preparations were completed, Tony LeVier initially flight-tested the first YF-94C. During its first and early later flights, stability and control problems were noted. These were subsequently corrected, and the airplane performed as advertised.

In December 1950, test pilot Herman R. ("Herm" or "Fish") Salmon of Lockheed dived YF-94C number one from 45,000 feet and attained supersonic speed as he passed through 33,000 feet; Flight Test Engineer Glen Fulkerson was in the rear cockpit, thereby becoming the first-ever supersonic passenger. The F-94 Starfire became the first straight-winged airplane to exceed the speed of sound, other than Bell's X-1—a purely experimental research aircraft, air launched and powered by a four-chamber rocket motor with 6,000 pounds of thrust.

Of his earlier experience on the original YF-94 service test airplane, LeVier reported in a letter to the author: "I don't believe the YF-94 was as fast as the F-80 or would climb as fast except when the afterburner was used, and of course that made a big difference. With afterburner on, the YF-94 would bump its critical Mach number, which was 0.8 Mach."

Another proposed version of the Starfire was the YF-94D model, which was to be optimized for the ground-support role. It was to be used in the Korean War and incorporated an awesome array of firepower comprising eight nose-mounted .50 caliber machine guns, two 1,000 pound bombs, and sixteen 5 inch diameter high-velocity aircraft rockets. It was to be a single-seat airplane powered by a higher-thrust version of the J48 engine. A pair of YF-94D service test aircraft, for aerodynamic and armament evaluation, were created from two production F-94Bs. A production contract for 112 F-94Ds followed but was canceled because of the delays associated with the F-97A—cum—F-94C program.

The F-94A, -94B, and -94C Starfire aircraft were interim all-weather fighters that filled the void until better types appeared. In all, not counting service test examples, Lockheed manufactured some 850 production Starfires in three versions. Not bad. In fact, impressive.

YF-94 Specifications

Type	Tandem-seat, single-engine service test all-weather fighter-interceptor
Wingspan	38 feet, 11 inches
Wing area	234.8 square feet
Length	40 feet, 1 inch
Height	12 feet, 8 inches
Empty weight	10,000 pounds
Maximum weight	13,000 pounds
Maximum speed	600 miles per hour
Service ceiling	45,500 feet
Rate of climb	11,200 feet per minute
Maximum range	1,000 miles
Armament	4 .50 caliber machine guns; 1,200 rounds of ammunition
Powerplant	1 nonafterburning Allison J33-A-23 engine or 1 afterburning Allison J33-A-33 or -33A turbojet engine

YF-94B Specifications

Type	Tandem-seat, single-engine service test all-weather fighter-interceptor (improved)
Wingspan	38 feet, 11 inches
Wing area	234.8 square feet
Length	40 feet, 1 inch
Height	12 feet, 8 inches
Empty weight	10,064 pounds
Maximum weight	13,475 pounds
Maximum speed	600 miles per hour
Service ceiling	45,500 feet
Rate of climb	6,850 feet per minute
Maximum range	1,500 miles
Armament	4 .50 caliber machine guns; 1,200 rounds of ammunition
Powerplant	1 afterburning Allison J33-A-33A turbojet engine

YF-94C (Formerly YF-97A) Specifications

Type	Tandem-seat, single-engine service test all-weather, all-missile-armed fighter-interceptor (advanced)
Wingspan	42 feet, 5 inches
Wing area	388 square feet
Length	44 feet, 6 inches
Height	14 feet, 11 inches
Empty weight	12,700 pounds
Maximum weight	18,300 pounds

YF-94C (Formerly YF-97A) Specifications

Maximum speed	585 miles per hour (Mach 0.875)
Service ceiling	50,000 feet
Rate of climb	7,980 feet per minute
Maximum range	1,250 miles
Armament	24 2.75 inch unguided Mighty Mouse rockets; production F-94Cs carried 48 rockets
Powerplant	1 afterburning Pratt & Whitney J48-PW-5 turbojet engine

YF-94, YF-94B, YF-94C, and YF-94D Production

Model Number	Designation	Serial Number	Comments
780- -	YF-94-00-LO	48-356	
780- -	YF-94-00-LO	48-373	
780-76-12	YF-94B-00-LO	49-2497	
880- -	YF-94C-00-LO	50-955	Originally carried civil registration number N94C and was developed under Temporary Design Number L-188
880- -	YF-94C-00-LO	50-877	
980-75-14	YF-94D-00-LO	51-5500	
980-75-14	YF-94D-00-LO	51-5501	

Chapter 6

XF-90 Penetration Fighter

After evaluating all three planes submitted in the competition for a penetration fighter, the Air Force decided against putting any of them into production. All offered about the same performance, but none met the requirement sufficiently to warrant a production order. Actually, the World War II concept of an all-purpose fighter plane was already obsolete when the XF-90 flew [June 1949].

—Tony LeVier

During World War II in Europe, the U.S. Army Air Forces used piston-powered, propeller-driven Lockheed P-38 Lightnings, Republic P-47 Thunderbolts, and North American P-51 Mustangs for its long-range bomber escort–fighter requirements. Although they were effective in the safeguarding of contemporary bomber aircraft, these three classic fighter aircraft would not be capable of protecting the U.S. Army Air Forces' upcoming postwar jet-powered bomber aircraft. Therefore, a requirement for a jet-powered bomber escort–fighter came about, and on 28 August 1945, the U.S. Army Air Forces Air Materiel Command invited design proposals from the industry for what it called a penetration fighter. The first

requirements for this proposed fighter were as follows:
- A single-place cockpit with a bubble-type cockpit canopy
- A twin-engine, turbojet propulsion system
- Sweptback flying surfaces
- Either six .50 caliber machine guns or six 20 millimeter cannons with provision for external stores—fuel tanks, bombs, and rockets
- A 600 miles per hour maximum speed at best altitude
- A 10-minute time to climb to 35,000 feet and a 40,000 foot service ceiling
- A 900 mile combat radius with a full combat load and a system stressed for 7.33g

But even before the ink had dried on this list, a series of performance changes were made:

the combat radius with a full combat load was increased to 1,500 miles and then decreased to 600 miles; the service ceiling was raised to 45,000 feet; and the time to climb was lowered to 4.9 minutes, but the altitude was increased to 50,000 feet. These changing requirements created many obstacles for Skunk Works

preliminary design group, directed by Project Engineers Don Palmer and Bill Ralston under the watchful eyes of Chief Research Engineer Kelly Johnson.

These demands dictated that Lockheed design a very large and heavy fighter airplane capable of carrying a vast amount of internal fuel, either six machine guns or six

Rare Skunk Works experimental shop view of a full-scale engineering mockup of the XP-90. Lockheed

cannons with their related ammunition and so on, and external stores such as auxiliary fuel tanks, bombs, and unguided air-to-ground rockets. Moreover, as a penetration fighter, it was to pull double duty as (1) a long-range bomber escort–fighter maneuverable enough to fend off attacking enemy interceptors and (2) a long-range fighter-bomber able to attack ground targets. Clearly, in 1945, the design of such a plane was a formidable task—especially since contemporary turbojet engines were not very powerful, not very reliable, and not very fuel efficient. Nonetheless, Lockheed responded to the U.S. Army Air Forces' invitation to bid; the proposal was due by 31 October 1945.

On 15 October 1945, the proposal for Lockheed Temporary Design Number L-153 was submitted to the U.S. Army Air Forces Air Materiel Command for evaluation in the penetration fighter competition. Two days earlier, McDonnell proposed its Model 36. Both proposals were approved for further development, and all other contenders were eliminated. Both firms received

The roll-out of the first XF-90. Its very clean lines are apparent in this overhead view. Lockheed

*Inflight view of XF-90 number one after
installation of its wing tip fuel tanks;*
Tony LeVier is under the canopy.
Lockheed

letter contracts in June 1946 for two flyable airplanes, a full-scale engineering mockup, wind tunnel models, and engineering data; the first flight was to occur by 31 October 1948. McDonnell's entry was designated XP-88, and Lockheed's challenger received the designation XP-90.

Lockheed's Skunk Works spent nearly two years in preliminary design working up its proposed penetration fighter. Before the design of Temporary Design Number L-153 was frozen, some sixty-five different configurations were investigated. There were sweptback V- or butterfly-tail designs with sweptback wings; delta-wing designs with sweptback horizontal or vertical tails; three-engine designs, with one engine on either wing tip and one in the fuselage; and even a design with a W-shaped wing planform. Finally, in early 1947, Lockheed settled on a Kelly Johnson masterpiece for appearance.

Lockheed's Temporary Design Number L-153 design featured a long, sleek fuselage with a single-place cockpit and two tail-mounted J34 axial-flow turbojet engines, fed air by means of cheek-type engine air inlets on either side of the fuselage. All of its flying surfaces were sweptback, and both the vertical and horizontal tail planes had a variable-geometry feature whereby their sweepback

Owing to its high weight and low power, the XF-90 needed great runway distances to take off. With rocket-as-sisted takeoff units, takeoff distance was reduced substantially. Lockheed

and incidence, could be altered during flight.

The Air Materiel Command approved Lockheed's Temporary Design Number L-153 air vehicle design and ordered two prototype XP-90s, a static test article, a full-scale engineering mockup, wind tunnel models, and engineering data on 20 June 1946; then, Temporary Design Number L-153 became Model 090-32-01.

For some reasons that remain unclear, McDonnell's Model 36 (XP-88) design moved to the

hardware stage some ten months sooner than Lockheed's XP-90: the XP-88 mockup was ready for inspection first, XP-88 number one rolled out first, and the airplane flew first. Nevertheless, Lockheed moved forward on the project.

The U.S. Air Force 689 Engineering Board inspected Lockheed's XF-90 (XP-90 before 11 June 1948) mockup during 4–8 April 1949. It was approved. By this time, the first airplane was nearing completion; the second was about half finished.

Both XF-90s flying side by side before their wing tip fuel tanks were fitted; the number two XF-90 is in the foreground. Lockheed

By the time XF-90 number one was completed and trucked to Muroc Army Air Field in early May 1949, both of McDonnell's XF-88 Voodoos were flying. In fact, XF-88 number one had already been flying for some seven months.

After the usual ground tests and evaluations, including low- and medium-speed taxi trials to check steering, braking, and so on, XF-90 number one was ready for flight. Again, Tony LeVier would serve as chief test pilot.

On the morning of 3 June 1949, LeVier rotated and piloted XF-90 number one up and away from Rogers Dry Lake. As predicted, though, getting only 6,000 pounds of total thrust from its two interim Westinghouse J34-WE-11 engines, the plane gave a performance that was less than spectacular; it was to fly with J34-WE-15 engines having 4,200 pounds of afterburning thrust, for a total thrust output of 8,400 pounds.

In an effort to move faster in obtaining the afterburner-equipped J34-WE-15 engines for the XF-90, Lockheed worked closely with Westinghouse and Solar. Lockheed provided XP-80A number two as an engine testbed, Westinghouse provided the J34-WE-15, and Solar developed the afterburner section. After testing, the YJ34-WE-15 engine with afterburner was cleared for use on the XF-90.

Lockheed proposed an RF-90 version, as shown here, with a model having a transparent nose section to show reconnaissance cameras. Lockheed

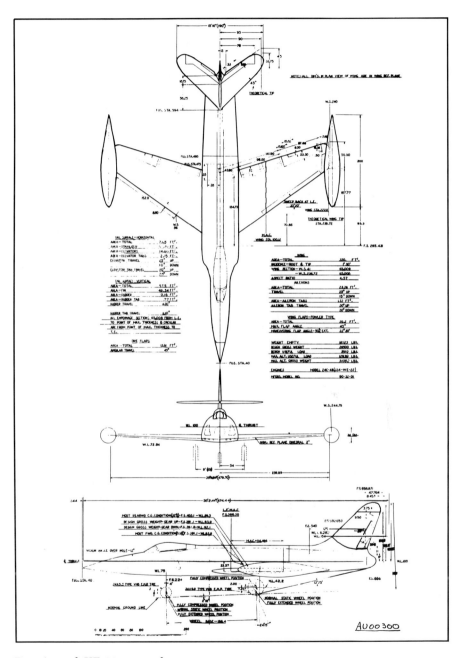

Drawing of XF-90 general arrange-
ment. Lockheed

On 17 May 1950, with YJ34-WE-15 engines, LeVier dived XF-90A (as redesignated with afterburning engines) number one to a maximum speed of Mach 1.12 during a series of speed trials that were run between 1 and 20 May 1950; this was done fifteen times.

Of the type's overall performance, LeVier reported in a letter to the author:

> The XF-90's general performance was very poor. It wasn't a helluva lot better with afterburner. The plane would have had a good chance for success had it had good engines, which it didn't. The aircraft was the only one in the competition that met U.S. Air Force specifications in regard to structural strength [it was stressed for 12.5g], so it was much heavier than the other contenders. The XF-90 was the third [combat fighter–type] plane in the world to dive supersonic. The plane was also strong as hell; you could not overstress it in flight.

A penetration fighter fly-off competition was held between 29 June and 7 July 1950 at Edwards Air Force Base. Seven U.S. Air Force pilots took part in the evaluation. The nine-day event was essentially over before it started, as by now, the penetration fighter program had been terminated by the Air Force.

Operations on the penetration fighter program were suspended at Edwards on 28 August 1950. A letter from the Air Materiel Command dated 11 September 1950 informed Lockheed that McDonnell's XF-88A Voodoo had been ranked number one of the three aircraft tested (a late entry, the North American YF-93A, was judged last). Lockheed therefore terminated the development of its XF-90 that same month.

The XF-90, however, proved to be a valuable learning tool for the Skunk Works. It taught Advanced Development Projects that it can lose as well as win. In other words, it made Kelly Johnson and his Advanced Development Projects teammates work even harder in the future. The result: continued Skunk Works success.

XF-90 Specifications

Type	Single-seat, twin-engine, long-range day fighter
Wingspan	40 feet
Wing area	345 square feet
Length	56 feet, 2 inches
Height	15 feet, 9 inches
Empty weight	18,050 pounds
Maximum weight	31,060 pounds
Maximum speed	668 miles per hour (Mach 1.12 attained in dive)
Service ceiling	39,000 feet
Rate of climb	5,555 feet per minute
Maximum range	2,300 miles
Armament	6 20 millimeter cannons
Powerplant	2 afterburning Westinghouse YJ34-WE-15 turbojet engines; originally, 2 nonafterburning Westinghouse YJ34-WE-11 turbojet engines

Note: The XF-90 was originally designated the XP-90 and was redesignated the XF-90A after the installation of afterburning engines.

XF-90 Production

Model Number	Designation	Serial Number
090-32-01	XF-90-00-LO	46-687
090-32-01	XF-90-00-LO	46-688

Note: XF-90A-2 was shipped to the NASA-Lewis Research Center, Cleveland, Ohio, in 1953 and was purposely destroyed during structural loads testing. XF-90A-2 was destroyed on the ground in 1952 during an atomic bomb test at Frenchman's Flat, Nevada.

Chapter 7

X-7 and XQ-5 King Fisher

After preliminary design within the Skunk Works, the X-7 program was transferred to Lockheed Missile Systems Division. That division, forerunner of today's Lockheed Missiles and Space Company at Sunnyvale, California, got its start at Lockheed's Van Nuys, California, facility on 1 January 1954.

—Rich Stadler

With few exceptions, most types of propulsion systems for powered air vehicles had been fully investigated by the mid-1940s. Aero-thermodynamic duct (athodyd), or ramjet, engine development, however, was in its infancy. In November 1944, with the primary goal of developing the ramjet engine as a propulsion system for both airplanes and missiles, R. E. Marquardt formed the Marquardt Company in Van Nuys. The first result of Marquardt's effort was the creation of the first successful American ramjet to be placed in production, the Marquardt RJ30-MA-1, a 20 inch diameter subsonic unit that propelled the Martin KDM-1 Plover target drone for the U.S. Navy. This was followed by the RJ31-MA-1 for the U.S. Air Force.

By 1947, Marquardt had developed models C-30 and C-48, of 30 inch and 48 inch diameters respectively, with higher power. That year, two C-30s were attached to the wing tips of a Lockheed P-80A Shooting Star for flight trials. This was most likely the first piloted airplane in the world capable of flight on ramjet power alone, as its normal J33 turbojet propulsion unit was shut down entirely on several occasions. Test Pilot Herman Salmon of Lockheed made the first flight—on record at the Smithsonian Institution—and all subsequent ramjet flights on this airplane.

X-7

Earlier, in late 1946, a real interest in ramjet engine technology began to materialize—especially within the ranks of the

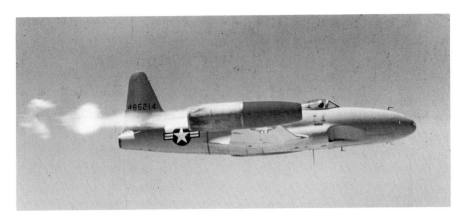

A P-80A with Marquardt 20 inch-diameter ramjet engines operating. Test pilot Herman R. ("Herm" or "Fish") Salmon of Lockheed is credited with making the first manned flight of an aircraft on *ramjet power—on record at the Smithsonian Institution. These ramjet engine tests were a prelude to those on the X-7 research missile and XQ-5 target drones. Lockheed*

U.S. Army Air Forces. On 6 December, the U.S. Army Air Forces opted to fund a pilotless air vehicle for both supersonic and hypersonic ramjet engine research under Secret Project MX-883. The proposed unmanned air vehicle, because it was to participate in dedicated research without any military application (where have we heard that before?), was given the designation X-7. A number of airframe contractors, including Lockheed—its Skunk Works especially—were given contracts, whereby a number of combination ramjet engine and air vehicle concept studies emerged. Lockheed settled on its Temporary Design Number L-171, which, in March 1947, was submitted to the U.S. Army Air Forces as a preliminary design for such an air vehicle; as directed by the U.S. Army Air Forces, it would also be used to test ramjet engines being developed by Wright Aeronautical. The Lockheed design won a contract in late 1948 when it entered into full-scale development.

The goal of the X-7 program, as defined in the Skunk Works' *Ramjet Vehicle Report No. 1* and reported by Roy Blay in the *Lockheed Horizons* article "Lockheed X-7 Ramjet Vehicle," was to "develop a flying testbed for any of several ramjet engines, capable of self-sustained flight between Mach 1.7 and 3, and at altitudes from sea level to 80,000 feet. The vehicle will be air-launched, boosted to flight speed, and recovered without damage via parachutes and ground-penetration spikes."

The Skunk Works' plan to recover these limited production air vehicles, without serious damage and for continued reuse, was unique for the day. This is how it worked: After the air vehicle's alloted fuel for the ramjet engine was gone (the ramjet engine, like the turbojet engine, burns various grades of jet propellant [JP] fuel) and the air vehicle had arrived over its planned recovery area, its parachute descent started. Nose-heavy at this point, owing to its design (it came equipped with a heavy nose-mounted ground-penetration spike), the air vehicle descended nose-down by way of a parachute until impact with the ground. If all went well, the air vehicle would land 90 degrees straight up-and-down with little or no structural damage to either the airframe or the powerplant. This recovery system worked well throughout the program.

Early launches of the X-7 were conducted from beneath the port wing of a modified Boeing B-29 Superfortress bomber at about

The first launch of an X-7 from a Boeing Superfortress. Note the smoking number four engine. Lockheed

30,000 feet. The X-7 then accelerated to supersonic speeds by way of either a single tail-mounted 105,000 pound thrust booster rocket or a pair of underwing-mounted 100,000 pound thrust booster rockets. Booster burnout time was about 5 seconds, by which point the underslung ramjet engine was functioning, and the booster unit or units, which incorporated large vertical and horizontal stabilizers (specifically the tail-mounted booster rockets), were automatically jettisoned from the principal air vehicle. Later versions of the X-7, including the XQ-5 King Fisher target drones, were launched from the bomb bay

A perfect 90-degree landing by means of a parachute descent and spike pene- *tration for X-7 missile recovery and reuse. Lockheed*

*An X-7 on permanent display at White
Sands Proving Ground, New Mexico.*
Lockheed

of a Boeing B-50 Superfortress II. Length was increased from 33 feet to 38 feet, and two underwing-mounted 50,000 pound thrust rocket boosters were employed instead of the tandem booster unit.

The telemetry developed by Skunk Works engineers to guide and control the X-7s and XQ-5s was the foundation of telemetry systems used today. Although the X-7's main mission was to test various ramjet engines, particularly that for the Boeing BoMarc ground-to-air interceptor missile, it also provided priceless data in the development of metal alloys, airframe structures, and instrumentation for future manned supersonic aircraft, especially the XF-104.

On 28 April 1951, the first X-7 was taken aloft under the left wing of a B-29. At an altitude of about 30,000 feet, it was released, and after a 5-second free fall, the booster rocket ignited. In rapid-fire sequence, as an early X-7 team member recalled in *Lockheed X-7 Ramjet Vehicle*, "things came unglued, and the bird became a group of separated flying parts." The B-29 managed to fly safely through it all.

Finally, on 7 May 1952, the first good flight of an X-7 came about, and the vehicle was safely recovered some 30 miles downrange; its spike nose recovery system worked to perfection.

From this time until the 130th and final flight in 1960, the Lockheed Skunk Works–developed X-7 broke all speed and altitude records for air-breathing air vehicles, recording best marks of Mach 4.31 and 106,000 feet.

The X-7 program was the nucleus for the Advanced Development Projects formation—

One of two XQ-5 drones. Lockheed

under Kelly Johnson's guidance—in 1953, of the Lockheed Missile System Division, which quickly outgrew its quarters at Lockheed's Burbank facility and, in 1954, moved to Van Nuys. Two years later, it moved again, to Sunnyvale, California, the present-day site of Lockheed Missiles and Space Company.

XQ-5 King Fisher

To create high-speed target drones in the mid-1950s, the Skunk Works produced two prototype XQ-5 King Fisher target drones for evaluation. Though they performed successfully, the U.S. Air Force elected to cancel the Q-5 program in favor of other, less expensive target drone types. It is strongly believed, but undocumented, that some X-7s were used as target drones in the late 1950s and early 1960s.

X-7A-1 Specifications

Type	Air-launched air vehicle designed for ramjet engine research
Wingspan	12 feet (21 feet, 5 inches on booster)
Wing area	90 square feet (approximate)
Length	33 feet (tail cone to spike nose tip; 46 feet with booster)
Height	7 feet (10 feet with booster)
Empty weight	4,300 pounds to 5,000 pounds (depending on ramjet engine)
Maximum weight	8,000 pounds to 8,800 pounds (depending on ramjet engine)
Maximum speed	Mach 4.31 (attained)
Service ceiling	106,000 feet (attained)
Rate of climb	Classified
Maximum range	Classified
Armament	None
Powerplant	Wright XRJ47-W-1 or -3; Marquardt XRJ43-MA-1, -3, -20B, -20C, -20XF1, -20XF4, -20XF6, -20XF8, -20XP1, -20XP3, -3, -20ZF5, -5, -20XF7, -20XF9, -7, or -20XS1; Marquardt XRJ43-MOD-11, -9, -20XS2, -11, or -20XS3; and Marquardt XRS59-MA-1, -24C, or -24D ramjet engines in 20 inch, 28 inch, and 36 inch diameters

XQ-5 Specifications

Type	Experimental target drone
Wingspan	10 feet
Wing area	60 square feet
Length	38 feet
Height	7 feet
Empty weight	4,300 pounds plus (depending on powerplant weight)
Maximum weight	8,000 pounds plus (depending on powerplant weight)
Maximum speed	Mach 3 plus
Service ceiling	100,000 feet plus
Rate of climb	Classified
Maximum range	100 miles plus
Armament	None
Powerplant	Many of the same ramjet engine–rocket booster propulsion units employed by X-7 missiles (see "X-7A-1 Specifications" chart)

X-7 (Also Known as X-7A-1) and XQ-5 Production

Designation	Serial Number	Designation	Serial Number
X-7A-00-LO	55-3167	X-7A-00-LO	57-6299
X-7A-00-LO	55-3168	X-7A-00-LO	57-6300
X-7A-00-LO	55-3169	X-7A-00-LO	57-6301
X-7A-00-LO	55-3170	X-7A-00-LO	57-6302
X-7A-00-LO	55-3171	X-7A-00-LO	57-6303
X-7A-00-LO	55-3172	X-7A-00-LO	57-6304
X-7A-00-LO	55-3173	X-7A-00-LO	57-6305
X-7A-00-LO	56-4045	X-7A-00-LO	57-6306
X-7A-00-LO	56-4046	X-7A-00-LO	57-6307
X-7A-00-LO	56-4047	XQ-5-00-LO	56-4054
X-7A-00-LO	56-4048	XQ-5-00-LO	58-1025
X-7A-00-LO	56-4049		
X-7A-00-LO	56-4050		
X-7A-00-LO	56-4051		
X-7A-00-LO	56-4052		
X-7A-00-LO	57-6295		
X-7A-00-LO	57-6296		
X-7A-00-LO	57-6297		
X-7A-00-LO	57-6298		

Note: Official U.S. Air Force contract records indicate that twenty-eight X-7As or X-7A-1s and two XQ-5s were built. It remains undocumented as to whether other X-7 types were built—namely, X-7A-3s and X-7Bs, as reported in other references.

Chapter 8

XF-104 Starfighter

If it hadn't of been for aircraft like the F-104, which was strategically targeted at key Russian facilities, and the U-2, which let us know everything the communists were doing, there may very well have been a World War III.

—Tony LeVier

One of the Skunk Works' most rewarding—indeed one of Kelly Johnson's most successful—ventures was in the creation of the record-setting, award-winning Lockheed F-104 Starfighter, which developed from the XF-104. Dubbed the Missile with a Man in It for obvious reasons, the rocketlike F-104 was designed from the outset to satisfy U.S. Air Force Korean War fighter pilots' criterion: specifically, to a person, they wanted and needed a pure daytime air superiority fighter that could outclass any fighter in the foreseeable future.

The conception of what became the F-104 Starfighter developed in the early days of the Korean War. On 1 November 1950, six sweptwing jet fighter planes came across the Yalu River and jumped a flight of World War II–era North American F-51 Mustang

fighters that were flying near the Manchurian border over North Korea. The piston-powered, propeller-driven Mustangs were no match for the new jet-powered MiG-15 fighters, which had just made their expected debut but much sooner than had been anticipated. Worse, all other fighter types in the theater of operations were likewise outclassed by the Russian-built MiG-15s being flown by North Korea's air force.

Even though sweptwing, jet-powered North American F-86 Sabre Jet fighters, which matched the MiG-15's aerial prowess, began arriving in South Korea in December 1950, no clear-cut fighter-to-fighter advantage existed. The only difference was better U.S. Air Force pilot training and skill. The MiG-15 had become a star overnight, and a new type of fighter—a star fighter—was needed to combat it.

U.S. Air Force fighter pilots, as they gained operational experience fighting MiG-15s, quickly formed definite ideas about the type of jet fighter plane that could gain and maintain local air superiority over Korea. Basically, they said, the fighter must trade weight and complexity for greater speed, maneuverability, and agility; it must have superior speed and altitude, it must be light and simple, and it must be able to

XF-104 number one at Edwards Air Force Base on 22 July 1954. Prompted by U.S. Air Force experience in the Korean War, and created by Kelly Johnson's famed Skunk Works design group, two Lockheed XF-104 Starfighter prototypes led to the answer to the high-performance MiG fighter series— MiG-15, MiG-17, MiG-19, and MiG-21. Department of Defense; Robert F. Dorr

XF-104 number one as it appeared in 1956 while it was serving as a chase plane for YF-104A flight test action. Two-port-opening cockpit canopy is noteworthy. U.S. Air Force

fly circles around its adversary aircraft.

The Skunk Works had been thinking along these same lines since early 1950, and a dedicated team of Advanced Development Projects engineers under Kelly Johnson came up with a provocative design for a jet fighter with very thin, straight wings. What they sought was a fighter that would be notable, even

Tony LeVier, while performing speed runs on XF-104 number one (shown), exceeded 1,000 miles per hour (Mach 1.5) shortly after this photograph was taken. He became the world's first 1,000 mile per hour pilot in a jet-powered aircraft. In a letter to the author he said, "The F-104 was a helluva fighter, but you had to know how to work it!" Lockheed

Both prototype XF-104s fly in formation. The first XF-104, foreground, has wing tip fuel tanks attached; the second XF-104 is clean. Lockheed

revolutionary, in design yet retain production and maintenance simplicity. The key Skunk Works engineers on the air superiority fighter program, in part, were

Ed Baldwin
Dick Boehme
Phil Colman
Henry Combs
Rus Daniell
Gene Frost
Willis Hawkins
R. Richard ("Dick") Heppe
James ("Jim") Hong
Bill Ralston
Ben Rich
John Stroud
Art Vierick

Ralston served as project engineer; Vierick—once more—was in charge of the shop. These thirteen engineers, under Hall Hibbard, chief engineer, and Kelly Johnson, assistant chief engineer and chief designer, were up to the task.

To get information from the horse's mouth—from U.S. Far East Air Force fighter pilots—Johnson toured South Korea in 1951; he covered more than 23,000 miles and visited fifteen air bases, flying in a U.S. Air Force Lockheed C-121 Constellation—another classic Johnson design.

When he returned from South Korea, Johnson began to design a jet fighter that would fly faster and higher than anything else flying in the world. The U.S. Air Force had no requirement for a dedicated air superiority fighter; however, that soon ended with Johnson's visit to the Pentagon. He showed his proposal to General Donald L. ("Don") Putt, commander of U.S. Air Force Systems Command from 30 June 1953 to 14 April 1954; General Don Yates; and Colonel Bruce Holloway. They were very taken with Johnson's unsolicited offering. But to get a contract, an official requirement for the plane had to materialize.

As Johnson recalled in his book *Kelly: More Than My Share of It All*, Colonel Holloway said: "Well, if there isn't a requirement, I'm going to make one. Stick around, Kelly. Come back in a couple of hours."

Colonel Holloway wrote up a set of requirements under Weapon System 303A, got authorization from Generals Putt and Yates, and handed it to Johnson. "Go see what you can do with this," Colonel Holloway told Johnson.

The specifications called for a pure air superiority day fighter with exceptional climb rate, speed, ceiling, agility, and maneuverability—a dogfighter in the truest sense of the word. The new and advanced lightweight fighter was to supplement, and ultimately replace, the North American F-100 Super Sabre beginning in 1956.

To obtain the best possible reliability and speed from its airframe, Lockheed chose to power its XF-104s with a single afterburning Wright J65-W-7 turbojet engine on an interim basis until the afterburning General Electric J79-GE-3 turbojet engine became available. Initially, though, only the nonafterburning Buick-built Wright J65-B-3 engine was available to the XF-104 flight test activities.

The Skunk Works subsequently met all U.S. Air Force standards for a high-performance lightweight fighter by designing an aircraft with an empty weight of just 11,500 pounds. It was a lean airplane, every ounce of extra weight being removed from its airframe and components. In fact, it was half the weight of the competitors' proposed Weapon System 303A aircraft. Moreover, Johnson's

XF-104 number two on its first flight with Tony LeVier under the canopy. Lockheed

design team had concentrated its efforts on a fighter plane with a high thrust-to-weight ratio to give it an advantage in the supersonic speed regime in which it would fly and fight. The Starfighter was win-win from the start, as it had beat out several otherwise good designs: the Northrop Model N-102 Fang, the North American Model NA-212 F-100B(I) Ultra Sabre, and the Republic Model AP-55 Thunderwarrior.

Under Weapon System 303A, the U.S. Air Force ordered a pair of XF-104 prototypes on 12 March 1953. The mockup was looked at and approved on 30 April, clearing the way for production of the two prototypes, beginning in

mid-1953. The first example was completed in secret in January 1954 with no roll-out party.

After being trucked to the secret North Base Area of Edwards Air Force Base and prepared for flight, the number one XF-104 made an unscheduled hop on 28 February 1954. Its official first flight, with Tony LeVier at the controls, was on 5 March. LeVier and Herm Salmon continued to demonstrate the Starfighter after

the arrival of XF-104 number two—number one being the aerodynamic testbed, number two being the armament testbed.

On 25 March 1955, powered by the afterburning J65-W-7, the number two XF-104 reached a top speed of Mach 1.79 (1,324 miles per hour) with test pilot Ray Goudey of Lockheed in control. On 18 April, Salmon was forced to eject because the ejection seat hatch on the floor blew out. With

Herm Salmon poses with an early F-104, circa 1956. "Flight falsies" (fairings over the General Electric J79's air inlets) were attached in an effort to hide the unique shock half cones in the inlets; the half cones helped reduce Mach 2 airflow into the J79 to Mach 0.7 for improved engine efficiency. Lockheed

Aerodynamicist R. Richard ("Dick") Heppe joined Lockheed in 1947. Very capable, Heppe was subsequently assigned to a series of engineering and general management positions that involved him in the conception and development of every new airplane proposed or produced since then. These included the XF-90, XF-104, YF- and F-104A, YC-130, SST, L-1011, S-3A, CP-140, and a number of rigid-rotor helicopters. In 1974, he became a vice-president of Lockheed Corporation. On 1 April 1984, Heppe became vice-president and general manager of the Skunk Works. Two months later, he was elected president of Lockheed-California Company. Lockheed

James Hong, former L-1011 TriStar program manager, participated in the aerodynamic analysis and design of the XF-104. Hong helped on the design of the F-104's unique T-tail configuration. Lockheed

sudden decompression, Salmon's pressure suit inflated, and he could not see what had happened. Believing he had experienced a gun-firing mishap, as LeVier had earlier, he ejected and landed safely, and XF-104-2 was lost.

Both XF-104s came equipped with the soon-to-be-unpopular downward-firing ejection seat system devised by Lockheed. The number two airplane was equipped with a single, rotary-action, six-barrel prototype General Electric M61 Vulcan 20 millimeter cannon. Both featured T-tails with all-movable stabilators (stabilizers and elevators) and thin, straight wings that were angled downward 10 degrees. The F-104 was such a new and unique design—radical, in ways—that it

111

soon earned the title Missile with a Man in It, owing to its rocketlike looks.

Seeing that the XF-104 proved successful, with interim power, the U.S. Air Force upped its order and procured seventeen service test YF-104As and six preproduction F-104As on 30 March 1955. And the saga of the famed F-104 Starfighter began.

The success of the XF-104s and YF-104As led to the production of 153 operational F-104As for service with both Aerospace Defense Command and Tactical Air Command, and ultimately led to the manufacture in the United States and abroad of 2,578 Starfighters for the U.S. Air Force and a number of foreign users.

XF-104 Specifications

Type	Single-seat, single-engine prototype daytime air superiority fighter
Wingspan	29 feet, 9 inches (without wing tip fuel tanks)
Wing area	196.1 square feet
Length	54 feet, 8 inches (without nose boom)
Height	13 feet, 5 inches
Empty weight	11,500 pounds
Maximum weight	25,000 pounds
Maximum speed	Mach 1.79 (attained)
Service ceiling	64,795 feet
Rate of climb	35,000 feet per minute
Maximum range	900 miles
Armament	1 rotary 6-barrel 20 millimeter General Electric M61 Vulcan cannon (XF-104 number 2 only)
Powerplant	1 nonafterburning Buick-built Wright J65-B-3 turbojet engine (XF-104 number 1 only); 1 afterburning Wright J65-W-7 turbojet engine (both XF-104s after number 1 was reengined)

XF-104 Production

Model Number	Designation	Serial Number	Comments
083-92-01	XF-104-00-LO	53-7786	Used as aerodynamic testbed
083-92-01	XF-104-00-LO	53-7787	Used as armament testbed

Chapter 9

XFV-1 Salmon

As far as risking my neck was concerned, that's what I was paid for. The way we approached the project, getting the airplane off the ground wasn't really too much different or dangerous than flying a conventionally configured aircraft.

——Herm Salmon

Named in memory of the only man to fly it, Chief Engineering Test Pilot Herman Salmon of Lockheed, the Lockheed XFV-1 Salmon was a proposed ship-based vertical-takeoff-and-landing convoy fighter for the U.S. Navy. In a winner-take-all fly-off competition with the Convair XFY-1 Pogo, the XFV-1, designed by Kelly Johnson and his Skunk Works, came in second-best. Although the Convair entry won, it did not prove to be successful enough to generate a production order. Thus, on 16 June 1955, the U.S. Navy's Convoy fighter program would be canceled.

In 1950, because of its growing concern about inadequate convoy defense during World War II—and adequate convoy defense in the 1950s and beyond—the U.S. Navy held a design competition for a relatively small and light VTOL

fighter to equip merchant ships for their own defense. Therefore, unlike those during World War II, naval warships of the future would be able to perform duties other than the defense of merchant ships. The idea was to create a tail sitter, or vertical riser, so that no runway would be needed—on land or at sea. With this, the convoy fighter program was born.

Lockheed and four other airframe contractors—Convair, Goodyear, Martin, and Northrop—responded and submitted their respective convoy fighter proposals. Goodyear and Northrop were eliminated early on. Convair's entry was preferred, as it was thought best suited for the mission; moreover, it was to cost less than the others. Lockheed and Martin were runners-up. Finally, Martin's entry was eliminated because Lockheed had quoted a

Herm Salmon joined Lockheed in 1940 to ferry Hudson bombers to Montreal in Canada. He tested P-38s and B-17s, did all the spin tests on the P-38, and did half the dive tests on the F-80, F-90, and F-94C. He did all Civil Aeronautics Administration (CAA) certification tests of the Constellation and Super Constellation (Models 649s and 1049s), made the first manned flight on ramjet engine power, did spin tests on the T-33, did all the flight tests on the XFV-1, made the first flight of the YF-104A, flew Federal Aviation Administration certification tests on the Electra, and conducted flight tests on the P3V (later P-3) Orion. He became chief engineering test pilot for Lockheed-California Company before his retirement in 1968 after 28 years of service. Born on 11 June 1913, he passed away on 22 June 1980 in the crash of his own Model 1049 Super Constellation. In his honor, since he was the only person to fly the XFV-1, Lockheed named it the Salmon. Lockheed

The vertical flight pioneer—the U.S. Navy Lockheed XFV-1—was designed to rise vertically, level off for 550 miles per hour horizontal flight, and land vertically on its tail wheels. The number one XFV-1 prototype poses vertically on its four tail wheels in this 1955 photograph. Lockheed

*Fish Salmon boards the number one
XFV-1 Salmon for a Lockheed publicity
photo.* Lockheed; Robert F. Dorr

lower price for its design. So, the convoy fighter competition was between Convair and Lockheed. Then, on 19 April 1951, both firms received similar contracts to produce two prototypes. Convair's prototype convoy fighter was designated XFY-1, and Lockheed's prototype was designated XFO-1 (shortly after contract award, the designation XFO-1 was changed to XFV-1).

Earlier, in August 1950, under Kelly Johnson's direction, Lockheed's Skunk Works initiated the design of Model 81; Art Flock served as project engineer. The Model 81 design featured four tail planes in an X-configuration with fully castering struts and wheels on each, a trapezoidal wing planform, and center-mount wing tip fuel tanks. The wing tip tanks, in addition to fuel, were initially to carry test equipment, and in the proposed production model, an armament of either forty-eight 2.75 inch-diameter folding-fin aircraft rockets or four 20 millimeter cannons, half on each tank. Lockheed, like Convair, elected to power its entry with the Allison

XFV-1 number one poses on its temporary, albeit final, landing gear arrangement, which allowed it to take off and land in a conventional manner. Lockheed; Robert F. Dorr

YT40-A-6 turboprop engine, which comprised dual Allison T38s spinning two contrarotating three-blade propellers.

For initial flight test activities, it was decided to fly the first XFV-1 in the conventional mode only, because its interim T40-A-6 engine of 5,850 horsepower—offering only a 1.2:1 power-to-engine-weight ratio—was not expected to make the XFV-1 capable of continuous operation in the vertical mode. To do this, Lockheed engineered an interim

arrangement of nonretractable landing gear with fixed tail wheels attached to its two lower tail planes a la a tail dragger.

On 9 November 1953, XFV-1 number one was completed, then trucked to Edwards Air Force Base to undergo preflight ground tests and taxi tests. On 23 December, during a high-speed taxi test, a slight unscheduled liftoff occurred. Herm Salmon quickly reduced power and landed. Many more ground tests were conducted during the next six months, and

Herm Salmon sits in the cockpit of the XFV-1 as it rotates to the vertical on its special transport trailer, circa 1954. U.S. Navy; Robert F. Dorr

finally, on 16 June 1954, Salmon conducted the first official flight.

Salmon flew the XFV-1 another thirty-one times, totaling about 23 flying hours. Neither Lockheed nor Convair ever got its desired versions of the T40 engine. Thus, no maximum-performance tests came about for either contractor.

By June 1955, after months of continued disappointments on its convoy fighter program, the U.S. Navy canceled it. Worse for Lockheed, its entry never made a VTOL demonstration—as the Convair entry had done a number times—flying conventionally on all thirty-two of its flights.

Lockheed's proposed production version of the prototype XFV-1 was its Model 181 or FV-2, to be powered by the more powerful and reliable Allison T54-A-16 turboprop engine. It featured radar in the forward nonspinning propeller spinner, armor, and a bullet-proof windscreen.

Following the cancellation of the convoy fighter program, XFV-1 number one was delivered to Hiller Helicopters, Palo Alto, California, for ground tests on later Hiller VTOL air vehicle projects. XFV-1 number two was never completed.

It is rare indeed when a design out of Lockheed's Skunk Works fails. Especially a Kelly Johnson design. In this case, it happened as a result of an inadequate propulsion system and a flawed concept and not because the XFV-1 was unworthy of flight; it flew well. In the final analysis, Lockheed's XFV-1 Salmon was one

XFV-1 number one on its first flight at Edwards with a Lockheed T-33A chase plane alongside. Tremendous engine torque was partially eliminated with its two large-diameter contrarotating three-blade propellers. U.S. Air Force

of the many important steppingstones on the path to making VTOL aircraft work. For this reason, the XFV-1 lives on as a main attraction in a noted aviation museum—the Naval Aviation Museum, Naval Air Station Pensacola, Florida.

XFV-1 Specifications

Type	Single-seat, single-engine experimental VTOL convoy fighter
Wingspan	30 feet, 10⁷/₆₄ inches (with wing tip fuel tanks)
Wing area	246 square feet
Length	36 feet, 10$\frac{1}{4}$ inches
Height	same as length (sitting vertical)
Empty weight	11,599 pounds
Maximum weight	16,221 pounds
Maximum speed	580 miles per hour at 15,000 feet (estimated)
Service ceiling	43,300 feet (estimated)
Rate of climb	10,820 feet per minute (initial, estimated)
Maximum range	Unknown (estimated endurance was 1 hour and 10 minutes)
Armament	Either 4 20 millimeter cannons or 48 2.75 inch folding-fin aircraft rockets, as had been proposed
Powerplant	1 Allison XT40-A-6 turbine-propeller engine; the proposed production FV-2 was to be powered by 1 Allison T54-A-16

XFV-1 Production

Model Number	Designation	Bureau Number	Comments
081-40-01	XFV-1-00-LO	138657	On display at the Naval Aviation Museum Naval Air Station Pensacola, Florida.
081-40-01	XFV-1-00-LO	138658	Never-flown; now gate guardian at Naval Air Station Los Alamitos, California; some of its interior was never completed.

Chapter 10

YC-130 Hercules

It's rare indeed when the Navy procures an Air Force plane and vice versa. But in the case of the C-130, no naval aviator I know of ever scoffed at it. It's that good.

—Lt. Cmdr. Michael Brotherton, USN (retired)

On 15 May 1992, the Lockheed C-130 Hercules airlifter set yet another aviation milestone: 2,000 were built in over thirty-five years of continuous production. The two thousandth production Hercules— a C-130H—was delivered in a ceremony to the Kentucky Air National Guard. In production at Lockheed Aeronautical Systems Company, Marietta, Georgia, the Herk, or Herky Bird, if you prefer, is employed by all branches of the U.S. Armed Forces except the U.S. Army. Designed by Kelly Johnson and his Skunk Works, the C-130 is the finest tactical airlifter the world has known. In fact, the first production C-130A that was delivered to the U.S. Air Force in 1956 is still in operation today.

U.S. Air Force Far East Combat Cargo Command action in the Korean War dictated that a new tactical cargo and troop transport aircraft was badly needed to supplement, then replace, World War II–era Curtiss C-46 Commandos, Douglas C-47 Skytrains, and even the Fairchild C-119 Packet, which had just begun its U.S. Air Force career several months before the Korean War erupted.

To this end, on 2 February 1951, the U.S. Air Force sent requests for proposals to Boeing, Douglas, Fairchild, and Lockheed, with a detailed general operational requirement. According to René Francillon's *Lockheed Aircraft Since 1913*, this requirement for a medium tactical transport, in part, read as follows:

- Transport ninety paratroops 2,000 miles, or 30,000 pound cargo over a shorter range.
- Operate over unprepared and/ or short runways.
- Paradrop at no more than 187 miles per hour; fly even slower for *assault* landings.

On 2 July 1951, after a short-lived and very intense fight with

The number two Lockheed YC-130 Hercules service test airplane lifts off on its first flight out of Lockheed Air Terminal on 23 August 1954. Afterwards, it landed at Edwards Air Force Base for ongoing tests. Lockheed

Excellent inflight view of YC-130 number two after retracting its landing gear for the first time. The Hercules was designed for tasks as tough as those performed by its mythological namesake. Meeting military requirements, production C-130s operate from short runways with personnel or supplies or both while flying higher and faster than their contemporary military transports; C-130s drop paratroopers and airdrop cargo to ground troops, land on makeshift airstrips in front-line deliveries, evacuate wounded personnel, and carry troops or cargo or both on long-range logistic missions. Lockheed

Boeing, Douglas, and Fairchild, Lockheed was declared the hands-down winner of the U.S. Air Force competition to produce a new medium-sized logistic and tactical military transport that was to replace piston-powered medium transports then in service. At this time, Lockheed was awarded a contract to build two examples of a service test medium transport designated YC-130 and named Hercules. These were to be the U.S. Air Force's first purpose-built airlifters.

Under the supervision of Willis Hawkins, chief preliminary design engineer, and Art Flock, project engineer, Lockheed's Skunk Works designed Temporary Design Number L-206 (later Model 082) to exceed, or at least meet, the U.S. Air Force's exacting requirements. It featured a cargo compartment that was 41 feet, 5 inches long, 10 feet wide, and 9 feet high, with a total volume of 4,500 cubic feet, a rear loading ramp, and a spacious cockpit for two pilots, a navigator, a flight engineer, and a loadmaster. It had a high shoulder wing for easier loading and unloading, and its cargo floor was high enough to match the height of truck beds. Lockheed decided it would have four engines instead of two, as had been required. It would have four 3,250 shaft horsepower Allison T56-A-1 propjet engines spinning three-blade propellers.

Following a successful series of full-scale engineering mockup

inspections, Lockheed initiated construction of the two YC-130 service test aircraft at Burbank in mid-1953. The first example would serve as a static test article, to be flown after YC-130 number two. Completed in July 1953—two years after the contract award— YC-130 number two was rolled out and moved to the Lockheed flight line at Lockheed Air Terminal for a series of ground evaluations and taxi tests.

On 23 August 1954, with test pilots Stanley Betz (pilot) and Roy Wimmer (copilot), both of Lockheed, at its controls, YC-130 number two made a successful first flight, after which it was landed at Edwards Air Force Base for ongoing flight testing and evaluation.

Earlier, on 10 February 1953, the U.S. Air Force placed its first production order for seven C-130As. Still earlier, in 1952, after Lockheed convinced the U.S. Air Force that it should produce all C-130 airlifters at its new Marietta plant, most of the C-130 design team moved to Georgia; the C-130 project engineer was now Al Brown.

After YC-130 number one made its first flight, the YC-130 service test aircraft showed performance much better than had been specified by the U.S. Air Force; that is, top speed, cruising speed, rate-of-climb, service ceiling, and range figures were higher than original performance

After static tests, service test YC-130 number one made its first flight following YC-130 number two. The 12th production C-130A—very similar to the YC-130s—is shown on a test hop out of Lockheed's Marietta, Georgia, plant in 1955. Lockheed

projections. The U.S. Air Force was happy, and orders for many additional C-130s were quickly forthcoming.

The first production C-130A made its first flight at Marietta on 7 April 1955. Since then, many versions of the C-130 Hercules—including Models 382, 382B, 382E, and 382F and the L-100, L-100-20, and L-100-30 civil transport versions—have been purchased.

Indeed, the Lockheed C-130 Hercules has proved its ability time and time again. Designed in Lockheed's Skunk Works and built at Lockheed's Marietta plant, it's the best tactical airlifter the world has known. Who knows just how many more will be ordered and built in the future.

YC-130 Specifications

Type	4-engine service test medium-sized tactical military transport aircraft
Wingspan	132 feet, 6 inches
Wing area	1,745.5 square feet
Length	97 feet, 8 inches
Height	38 feet, 5 inches
Empty weight	58,769 pounds
Maximum weight	124,200 pounds
Maximum speed	383 miles per hour at 20,400 feet
Service ceiling	41,300 feet
Rate of climb	2,570 feet per minute
Maximum range	Unknown
Armament	None
Powerplant	4 Allison T56-A-1 turboprop engines

YC-130 Production

Model Number	Designation	Serial Number
082-44-01	YC-130-00-LO	53-3396
082-44-01	YC-130-00-LO	53-3397

Chapter 11

JetStar

Lockheed gambled six million of its own funds and gave Kelly Johnson and the Skunk Works the job of building two prototypes to meet the UCX specifications. Design work began in January 1957, and the new transport flew on 4 September—241 days later.

—*Roy Blay*

In early 1956, the U.S. Air Force notified airframe and powerplant contractors that it planned to procure flight-proven utility trainer experimental (UTX) and utility cargo experimental (UCX) aircraft to meet its need to modernize its old World War II–era utility transports and utility trainers.

At the time, however, the U.S. Air Force did not have the monies to fund either a UTX or UCX program. Thus, if contractors wanted potential future business, their UTX and UCX design, development, production, and flight testing would have to be funded with their own monies.

Three United States airframe contractors opted to develop the UTX and UCX prototypes with in-house funds. North American Aviation went after the UTX. The UCX was tackled by both

McDonnell Aircraft and Lockheed Aircraft. To keep its UCX design secret, Lockheed developed its entry within its classified Skunk Works.

Lockheed management gave Kelly Johnson's Skunk Works a go-ahead on the UCX program in December 1956. In January 1957, Johnson's preliminary design team began its work on CL-329 (*CL* meaning California-Lockheed).

Rolled out at Burbank on 1 August 1957, the first of a pair of prototypes, now named JetStar, with civil registration number N329J, was initially flight-tested at Lockheed Air Terminal on 4 September; it was landed at Edwards for additional flight test activities. Amazingly, it had flown only 241 days after preliminary design had started, and some nineteen months before its competitor from McDonnell! The

The number one JetStar prototype with Bristol Orpheus turbojet engines, circa 1962, after it was repainted and fit- ted with midwing 565 gallon slipper-type fuel tanks for extended range. Lockheed

Every good airplane design finds work. This JetStar was equipped with an electronic variable stability and control system in 1976 which allowed the airborne simulation of a wide variety of advanced aircraft. Called the General Purpose Airborne Simulator, the modified JetStar airplane had an advantage over ground-based simulators in that it provided motion and visual cues to its pilots while they were in a real-time flight environment. NASA's General Purpose Airborne Simulator JetStar-NASA 14, later N814NA, is the third production JetStar 6 model and has been extensively used by NASA's Ames/Dryden Flight Research Facility to study aircraft ride characteristics in flight. Eighty JetStar 6s were produced. NASA

second JetStar prototype was first flown on 15 March 1958. In 1958, in a demonstration by Lockheed to help increase sales, JetStar number two flew 6,700 miles in an 18-hour multistop tour of U.S. Air Force air bases.

On 31 October 1958, the U.S. Air Force announced that it would buy the JetStar—not as a utility cargo plane, but rather as a utility trainer plane, designated T-40A. It changed its mind, however, and ordered North American T-39s instead.

Finally, in 1959, the U.S. Air Force ordered an initial batch of five production C-140A JetStars. Then the U.S. Navy ordered two JetStar aircraft with the designation UV-1. From these humble beginnings, another 197 JetStars were built at Lockheed's Marietta plant; only the two prototypes were built in Burbank.

The JetStar was less costly than the McDonnell Model 119 or 220 entries; thus, neither McDonnell model was ordered or produced. Having built two prototypes, McDonnell had gambled on the UCX program, as Lockheed had, but lost.

UCX (JetStar Prototype) Specifications

Type	Twin-engine utility cargo experimental aircraft
Wingspan	53 feet, 8 inches
Wing area	523 square feet
Length	58 feet, 10 inches
Height	20 feet, 6 inches
Empty weight	15,139 pounds
Maximum weight	38,841 pounds
Maximum speed	613 miles per hour
Service ceiling	NA
Rate of climb	6,400 feet per minute
Maximum range	Unknown
Armament	None
Powerplant	2 nonafterburning Bristol Orpheus 1/5 turbojet engines

Note: *Wright was to build Orpheus engines in the United States under license as the TJ37 Orpheus.*

UCX (JetStar Prototype) Production

Model Number	Designation	Serial Number
CL-329	UCX	N329J
CL-329	UCX	N329K

Now wearing N814NA (formerly NASA 14) and a new paint scheme, NASA's Lockheed JetStar 6 continued to provide valuable in-flight data for many years that included: evaluation of wing coating and cleaning devices; laminar-flow control systems; and pylon-mounted propeller-fans. NASA

U-2 Dragon Lady

Be quick, be quiet, be on time

—Kelly Johnson

On 1 May 1960, while overflying the republic of Russia within the Union of Soviet Socialist Republics (USSR) (now the Commonwealth of Independent States), U.S. Air Force lieutenant Francis Gary ("Frank") Powers' U-2C was shot down near Sverdlovsk by a surface-to-air missile that detonated close by. Operational since June 1956, flown with impunity for forty-seven months, the U-2 had suddenly become vulnerable to radar-guided surface-to-air missiles. Worse, with Russia's capture of Lieutenant Powers (who was sentenced to spend ten years in a Russian prison but was set free in February 1962 in exchange for a Russian spy) and the ensuing anti-American propaganda from President Nikita Khrushchev of Russia, President Dwight D. Eisenhower of the United States was forced to forbid overflights of Russia by U-2s. Flights over China, however, continued in the early 1960s because China's surface-to-air missiles were less sophisticated. But the story of the Dragon Lady, the U-2, neither starts nor ends here.

Project Bald Eagle

In the late 1940s, Russia began testing nuclear bombs and in the early 1950s began developing manned and unmanned weapon systems to deliver them. These worrisome activities compelled the Department of Defense to issue *Design Study Requirement Number 53WC-16507*, dated 27 March 1953, calling for a subsonic single-seat aircraft able to transport a 700 pound payload to altitudes higher than 70,000 feet and for distances of more than 3,000 miles. The proposed air vehicle, under Project Bald Eagle, was to perform a daytime photographic reconnaissance mission. It was to be unarmed, and it was not to incorporate an ejection seat!

Three airframe contractors, each receiving a design study requirement, responded to what was now a U.S. Air Force program. These included Bell, Fairchild, and Martin under Secret Project MX-2147. Bell and Fairchild proposed new designs, and Martin offered a long-wing version of its B-57 Canberra, designated RB-57. Martin's proposal, the easiest and least expensive to produce, was accepted on an interim basis while work on an ultimate aircraft went on.

Prototype U-2 Angel, U.S. Air Force serial number 56-6674, as it appeared in August 1955 at its flight test area on one of the many Nellis Air Force Base test ranges—probably Groom Lake. Slightly sweptback flying surfaces and "dainty" landing gears are of interest. Lockheed

Another view of the original Dragon Lady—Lockheed build number 341, Central Intelligence Agency article number 001. Lockheed

Oddly, with its excellent background in covert aircraft programs, Lockheed's Skunk Works had not been issued this top-secret requirement. This both surprised and upset Kelly Johnson. Privately, with in-house monies, the Skunk Works organization had been conducting preliminary design studies on such an aircraft: *Lockheed Report Number 9732, Temporary Design Number L-282.* Based on the company's XF-104 configuration, Lockheed's design

A pair of U-2s, Lockheed build numbers 368 and 389: respectively, a U-2A, U.S. Air Force serial number 56-6701, background, and a U-2D (modified from a U-2A), U.S. Air Force serial number 56-6722, foreground. Lockheed

Later view of U-2D 56-6672 after still another modification and application of black paint. Note the extended speed brakes and deflected flaps. Lockheed

featured a very long wing for very high-altitude operations at subsonic speed over very long distances. As designed, it was to be powered by a single General Electric J73 turbojet engine modified for high-altitude operation. Soon, however, Lockheed found that both the U.S. Air Force and the Central Intelligence Agency were dead set on using the Pratt & Whitney J57 for the high-altitude mission— period. The Skunk Works modified Temporary Design Number L-282 to use the J57, as the other Bald Eagle competitors had already done to their designs. In 1954, as an unsolicited entry, Johnson offered the Temporary Design Number L-282 air vehicle design to the U.S. Air Force and Central Intelligence Agency.

Since Martin had already won a contract to produce interim high-altitude RB-57s, the contest was now among Bell, Fairchild, and Lockheed. All designs were reassessed.

The U.S. Air Force, preferring Bell's Model 67 design, ordered twenty-eight aircraft, U.S. Air Force serial numbers 56-0522 through 56-0549, in September 1954; the first example was to fly some eighteen months later. To hide its true nature, it was given a pure research designation: X-16. Work on the X-16 proceeded. In the meantime, Project Bald Eagle had changed to Secret Project Aquatone.

Secret Project Aquatone

As Project Bald Eagle–cum–Secret Project Aquatone evolved, the Skunk Works organization almost completely redesigned Temporary Design Number L-282. With its new fuselage, it no longer resembled the F-104. In fact, its new configuration made it look more like a powered sailplane, or glider, than a dedicated photographic reconnaissance aircraft. This fact also worked in favor of Project Aquatone because (1) it did not look threatening, and (2) it truly looked the part of a

A trio of U-2s in various configurations flying in formation, circa 1958. Lockheed; Tony Landis

133

high-altitude weather observation and research aircraft.

Kelly Johnson's Aquatone design, created with only twenty-five other Skunk Works engineers, including Phil Colman, Gene Frost, and Ben Rich, was finally accepted by the Central Intelligence Agency—not the U.S. Air Force—on 9 November 1954. Art Vierick, as always, it seems, was in charge of the shop; the engineering staff ultimately grew to eighty-one. The U.S. Air Force stayed with its choice of Bell's X-16, and the Central Intelligence Agency favored Lockheed's much-revised design—for good reason.

As it happened, Johnson said the Central Intelligence Agency or the U.S. Air Force or both could have twenty airplanes with spares for about $22 million and have the first one airborne within eight months. According to the book *Kelly: More Than My Share of It All*, Lieutenant General Don Putt of the U.S. Air Force helped Lockheed's sales pitch enormously with the following statement: "He [Johnson] has proven it several times already—on the F-80 [XP-80], F-80A [XP-80A], and F-104 [XF-104]." Therefore, Lockheed's Skunk Works got the official go-ahead on Project Aquatone.

Once again, Johnson chose Tony LeVier to be chief test pilot. LeVier, testing XF-104s at the time, joined Project Aquatone in early 1955. He selected the pseudonym

Anthony Evans for security. Thus, at this time, the X-16 was being developed in the open, while the U-2 (for Utility-Two, to hide *its* true mission) was developed in secret.

With an initial order for one U-2 prototype and nineteen production U-2As—Central Intelligence Agency articles 001 through 020, Lockheed build numbers 341 through 360—work on what was nicknamed Kelly's Angel proceeded at Lockheed's Burbank facility.

In July 1955, the Ranch, a top-secret test site within the Nellis Air Force Base test range complex in Nevada, was declared ready for U-2 flight testing and evaluation. The first U-2 was taken apart, and at 4:30 A.M. on 24 July, Skunk Works personnel arrived at the plant to start loading the plane into a U.S. Air Force Douglas C-124 Globemaster for its flight to Nevada; Johnson and company followed in a U.S. Air Force Douglas C-47 Skytrain.

U-2

After reassembly, the official birth of the U-2 came about. On 4 August 1955, programmed taxi trials with Tony LeVier were to begin. Instead, the U-2's unprogrammed first flight occurred. LeVier first made a low-speed taxi. He then made a medium-speed taxi. The prototype was real light, and on his second taxi run, it unexpectedly lifted off the runway to some 35 feet before he even realized he was airborne. When he tried to land the aircraft, it refused. LeVier found out the hard way that the U-2 could fly with the engine at idle power! Finally, LeVier bounced it down for a landing and bent the aft landing gear somewhat.

The *official* first flight was scheduled for the morning of 8 August 1955, and for this happening, all Skunk Works workers, engineers, and executives were present. Moreover, both Central Intelligence Agency and U.S. Air Force customers were on hand. If all went well, a traditional party would follow.

LeVier made the official, and very successful, test hop to 35,000 feet that day. The party followed. By year's end, three production U-2As—Central Intelligence Agency article numbers 002, 003, and 004—had joined up with the U-2 prototype, and 70,000 foot altitudes were being attained on a regular basis. The U-2s performed so well, the Skunk Works was able

A number of modular payloads for U-2 aircraft are shown by a U-2R, circa 1979. Lockheed; Tony Landis

A U-2 departing the main runway at Edwards Air Force Base, circa 1966. Seen below is the second of two North American XB-70A Valkyrie aircraft.

Ironically, Lockheed's A-12–YF-12–SR-71 Blackbird series of aircraft effectively doomed the U.S. Air Force's B-70 bomber program. Lockheed

to produce an additional six aircraft over the twenty-plane order for the same monies by not using planned spares. In fact, it produced those six extra U-2s so efficiently, it gave back to the government some $2 million!

Flight test and evaluation activities went so smoothly in early 1956 that the U-2 became operational in June. Although known to be tracked by Russian radar, no U-2 was successfully fired on until 1 May 1960, when civilian Frank Powers of the Central Intelligence Agency (a former U.S. Air Force lieutenant) was shot down.

Throughout the remainder of the 1950s and into the early 1960s,

Lockheed's Skunk Works continued to improve its basic U-2A design. The result was eight U-2 versions:

● U-2A: Original version with the Pratt & Whitney J57-PW-37 or -37A turbojet engine

● U-2B: Proposed version only, as the U.S. Air Force did not buy it; a variation of the U-2A with a radar nose and an aft cockpit for the radar operator

● U-2C: A version of the U-2A with the Pratt & Whitney J75-PW-13B turbojet engine

● U-2CT: A tandem-place version of the U-2C used for pilot training and transition

● U-2D: A tandem-seat version of the U-2C with an instrument

operator's station in the Q-bay (equipment bay); used for both electronic and communication intelligence operations
● U-2E, -2F, and -2G: Test versions of the U-2C for carrier landings and takeoffs, equipped variously with inflight refueling gear for longer loiter time

In 1965, Lockheed proposed a revised U-2C, the U-2R (R for Revised), with an overt designation of WU-2C. With this identification, Lockheed believed, those that did not need to know about the U-2R would only think that it was a weather version of the U-2. Again, Lockheed's Skunk Works produced a winner.

U-2R

By the time production of the original models of the U-2 ended in 1968, development of the revised U-2R was well in hand within the Skunk Works. The aircraft featured a wingspan of 103 feet with a 1,000 square foot area instead of the 600 square foot area of the original U-2s. It was powered by a version of the J75-PW-13B turbojet engine that now delivered 20 percent more thrust, at 17,000 pounds. Its cockpit had

A U-2R (former TR-1A) at night at Beale Air Force Base with its pilot, who is ready to fly. Lockheed

been enlarged 45 percent for increased pilot comfort on long endurance missions. In addition, the U-2R had a number of other equipment improvements and a provision for better field maintenance.

The U-2R flies nearly 9 miles every minute (540 miles per hour) above 70,000 feet, and it searches 300 miles to the horizon; it finds any and all enemy radar and communications stations. It loiters as many as 10 hours. In one case, when the *Mayaguez* was captured by Cambodian forces in May 1975 and a communications satellite went out of service, one U-2R stayed at 70,000 feet and above for more than 27 hours during a three-day period while serving as a communications link for the U.S. Armed Forces.

A two-place version of the U-2R used to train pilots is the U-2RT.

Reconnaissance Star

To create still another version of the U-2R and U-2RT, Lockheed designed a dedicated tactical reconnaissance aircraft, which it unofficially dubbed Reconnaissance Star.

In 1980, the Skunk Works reopened the U-2 production line to meet a U.S. Air Force need for thirty-three TR-1A (now U-2R), two TR-1B (now U-2RT), and two NASA ER-2 (now U-2ER) aircraft.

In June 1981, Lockheed delivered the first one off the

This 34-year-old U-2C, NASA N709NA, which was operated by the NASA-Ames Research Laboratory, set 16 time-to-climb and altitude records in a series of flights at Edwards Air Force Base during a one-week period. It was retired on 1 May 1989 and placed on display at Robins Air Force Base in Georgia, where it resides today. Lockheed

line—a U-2ER—to NASA's Ames Research Center northwest of San Jose in California. U-2R and U-2RT (formerly TR-1A and TR-1B) deliveries to the U.S. Air Force began in September 1981 and ended in October 1989, within budget and ahead of schedule. New-type U-2R aircraft numbers six and seven, delivered in 1983, were tandem-seat pilot trainer versions designated U-2RTs.

Skunk Works engineers optimized the U-2R to accommodate interchangeable nose sections for varied missions, mission bay hatches, and instrument wing superpods, allowing the new model to carry nearly 4,000 pounds of sensors

U-2D 56-6721 was specially modified for test operations at Edwards Air Force Base's Air Force Flight Test Center; this aircraft is overall gloss white with red stripes. Lockheed

One of two U-2CT aircraft, 56-6953, of the 4029th Strategic Reconnaissance Training Squadron, which also has a pair of U-2RT (former TR-1B) aircraft. Lockheed

and experiments. Powered by a single Pratt & Whitney J75-PW-13B engine, the new U-2Rs cruise above 70,000 feet at more than 430 miles per hour. All operational U-2Rs, whether early or late versions, are being reengined with the General Electric F101-GE-F29, a derivative of the F118 used by B-2 stealth bombers, which produces 19,000 pounds of thrust.

Missionized to provide all-weather, day-or-night battlefield surveillance in support of U.S. and allied ground forces, advanced U-2Rs can identify targets and threats well behind enemy lines without penetrating enemy airspace; unrefueled, their range exceeds 3,000 miles.

The Air Combat Command's U-2R aircraft are operated by the 9th Reconnaissance Wing at Beale Air Force Base in California; one detached squadron operates from the Royal Air Force Base at Alconbury, north of London, England.

When the last U-2R was delivered in a ceremony on 3 October 1989, Vice-President Ben Rich of the Skunk Works said in

The second of two NASA U-2ER (former ER-2) Earth Resources aircraft, foreground, flies formation with NASA's U-2C near Golden Gate Bridge, San Francisco, California; both aircraft are stationed at Naval Air Station Moffett Field near San Jose. The U-2C set a number of time-to-climb and altitude records before its retirement in 1989. Lockheed

An early production U-2R, 68-10339, in overall flat-black dress. Original U-2Rs are some 13 feet longer than earlier U-2s and have wingspans some 23 feet wider. Lockheed

An excellent view of a U-2R (former TR-1A) near Beale Air Force Base shows off its superpods to good advantage. U-2Rs are some 40 percent larger than earlier U-2s. Note the electronics countermeasures blister on the right-hand wing trailing edge. Lockheed

the April 1991 *Lockheed Advanced Development Company Information Sheet*: "We can point with pride to the TR-1 [U-2R] program as a model of the defense procurement process. It has consistently remained within budget and ahead of schedule."

Today, the Skunk Works continues to support the U.S. Air Force fleet of U-2Rs—new and old—with upgrades, spare parts, and service.

Lockheed's Skunk Works will not say exactly how many U-2s—still operational, thus highly classified—were built other than those in the accompanying "Known U-2 Production" chart. But one thing is certain: the U-2R of today is a much-improved version of the original U-2 that flew in 1955.

U-2 and U-2A Specifications

Type	Single-seat, single-engine strategic and tactical reconnaissance aircraft
Wingspan	80 feet
Wing area	600 square feet
Length	50 feet
Height	15 feet
Empty weight	12,750 pounds
Maximum weight	21,272 pounds
Maximum speed	450 miles per hour at 65,000 feet
Service ceiling	70,000 feet plus
Rate of climb	Classified
Maximum range	Classified
Armament	None
Powerplant	1 nonafterburning Pratt & Whitney J57-PW-31A (formerly J57-PW-37) engine

Note: Most U-2A aircraft were redesignated U-2Cs after being reengined with higher-thrust Pratt & Whitney J75-PW-13B jet engines.

U-2C and U-2CT Specifications

Type	Single-seat, single-engine strategic reconnaissance aircraft; tandem-seat trainer
Wingspan	80 feet
Wing area	600 square feet
Length	50 feet
Height	15 feet
Empty weight	13,070 pounds
Maximum weight	22,542 pounds
Maximum speed	460 miles per hour at 65,000 feet
Service ceiling	65,000 feet to 70,000 feet plus
Rate of climb	Classified

Maximum range	Classified
Armament	None
Powerplant	1 nonafterburning Pratt & Whitney J75-PW-13B turbojet engine

U-2R and U-2RT (Formerly TR-1A and TR-1B) Specifications

Type	Single-seat, single-engine tactical reconnaissance aircraft; tandem-seat trainer
Wingspan	103 feet
Wing area	1,000 square feet
Length	62 feet, 9 inches (with standard nose)
Height	16 feet
Empty weight	15,500 pounds (without fitted superpods)
Maximum weight	41,300 pounds
Maximum speed	430 miles per hour plus
Service ceiling	70,000 feet plus
Rate of climb	Classified
Maximum range	Classified
Armament	None
Powerplant	1 nonafterburning Pratt & Whitney J75-PW-13B turbojet engine; being reengined with 1 nonafterburning General Electric F101-GE-F29 turbofan engine

A strange-looking U-2R (former TR-1A), 80-1071, with its C-Span III data-link radome antenna modification. Lockheed; Tony Landis

143

Close-up view of a U-2R (former TR-1A)
defines the moniker Dragon Lady.
Lockheed; Tony Landis

Known U-2 Production

Lockheed Build
Designation U.S. Air Force

Number	Serial Number	Comments
U-2 341	56-6674	Nicknamed *Angel*; Central Intelligence Agency article number 001; disposition unknown
U-2A 342	56-6675	Disposition unknown
U-2A 343	56-6676	Disposition unknown
U-2A 344	56-6677	Lost at Edwards Air Force Base
U-2A 345	56-6678	Disposition unknown
U-2A 346	56-6679	Disposition unknown
U-2A 347	56-6680	Displayed at National Air and Space Museum, Washington, D.C.
U-2A 348	56-6681	NASA N708NA; displayed at NASA-Ames Research Center, Naval Air Station Moffett, California
U-2A 349	56-6682	N709NA; displayed at Robins Air Force Base, Georgia
U-2A 350	56-6683	Lost while returning from overflight of Cuba
U-2A 351	56-6684	Disposition unknown
U-2A 352	56-6685	Disposition unknown
U-2A 353	56-6686	Disposition unknown

Kelly Johnson, designer of the U-2 and 30-something other noted Lockheed aircraft, poses with U-2A N803X, *which was used for ongoing Lockheed developmental testing in the 1960s. Lockheed*

U-2A 354	56-6687	Disposition unknown
U-2A 355	56-6688	Disposition unknown
U-2A 356	56-6689	Disposition unknown
U-2A 357	56-6690	Lost, Ben Hoa Air Base, South Vietnam
U-2A 358	56-6691	Located at People's Republic of China Military Museum, Beijing, China
U-2CT 359	56-6692	Located at Royal Air Force Alconbury, United Kingdom
U-2C 360	56-6693	Lost in Russia; Frank Powers' U-2
U-2A 361	56-6694	Lost at Del Rio, Texas
U-2A 362	56-6695	Disposition unknown
U-2A 363	56-6696	Lost at Del Rio, Texas
U-2A 364	56-6697	Lost at Del Rio, Texas
U-2A 365	56-6698	Lost at Del Rio, Texas
U-2A 366	56-6699	Lost in New Mexico
U-2A 367	56-6700	Disposition unknown
U-2A 368	56-6701	Displayed at Strategic Air Command Museum, Offutt Air Force Base, Nebraska
U-2A 369	56-6702	Lost at Del Rio, Texas
U-2A 370	56-6703	Lost at Davis-Monthan Air Force Base, Arizona
U-2A 371	56-6704	Lost at Del Rio, Texas
U-2A 372	56-6705	Disposition unknown

Test pilot William M. ("Bill") Park of Lockheed, who amassed more than 1,000 flight hours in U-2 aircraft, prepares to flight-test a U-2R. Lockheed

LIFT CANOPY HERE

Test pilot Art Peterson of Lockheed, who also flew more than 1,000 flight hours in U-2s, poses in the cockpit of an unclear version of a U-2. Lockheed

Lockheed Build Designation Number	U.S. Air Force Serial Number	Comments
U-2A 373	56-6706	Disposition unknown
U-2A 374	56-6707	Displayed at Del Rio Texas Museum, Laughlin Air Force Base
U-2A 375	56-6708	Disposition unknown
U-2A 376	56-6709	Disposition unknown
U-2A 377	56-6710	Lost
U-2A 378	56-6711	Lost October 1962 to surface-to-air missile over Cuba
U-2A 379	56-6712	Lost in Idaho
U-2A 380	56-6713	Lost in New Mexico
U-2A 381	56-6714	Displayed at Beale Air Force Base, California
U-2A 382	56-6715	Disposition unknown
U-2A 383	56-6716	Displayed at Davis-Monthan Air Force Base, Arizona
U-2A 384	56-6717	Disposition unknown
U-2A 385	56-6718	Disposition unknown
U-2A 386	56-6719	Lost in South America
U-2A 387	56-6720	Lost at Del Rio, Texas
U-2A 388	56-6721	Displayed at March Air Force Base Museum, California
U-2A 389	56-6722	Displayed at U.S. Air Force Museum, Wright-Patterson Air Force Base, Dayton, Ohio
U-2A 390	56-6723	Disposition unknown
U-2D 391	56-6951	Lost at Davis-Monthan Air Force Base, Arizona
U-2D 392	56-6952	Lost at Davis-Monthan Air Force Base, Arizona
U-2CT-2 393	56-6953	Modified U-2D; displayed at Air Force Flight Test Center Museum, Edwards Air Force Base, California
U-2D 394	56-6954	Lost at Davis-Monthan Air Force Base, Arizona
U-2D 395	56-6955	Lost

Known U-2R and U-2RT Production

Designation	Serial Number	Comments
U-2R-1	68-10329	
U-2R-2	68-10330	Also carried civil registration number N810X
U-2R-3	68-10331	
U-2R-4	68-10332	
U-2R-5	68-10333	

*U-2R (former TR-1A) 80-1067 without
superpods.* Lockheed

Designation	Serial Number	Comments
U-2R-6	68-10334	
U-2R-7	68-10335	
U-2R-8	68-10336	
U-2R-9	68-10337	
U-2R-10	68-10338	
U-2R-11	68-10339	Modified to U.S. Navy EP-X testbed
U-2R-12	68-10340	Modified to U.S. Navy EP-X testbed
U-2R-13	68-10341	
U-2R-14	68-10342	
U-2R-15	68-10343	
U-2R-16	68-10344	
U-2R-17	68-10345	
U-R	68-10346	Not proceeded with
U-R	68-10347	Not proceeded with
U-R	68-10348	Not proceeded with
U-R	68-10349	Not proceeded with
U-R	68-10350	Not proceeded with
U-R	68-10351	Not proceeded with
U-R	68-10352	Not proceeded with
U-R	68-10353	Not proceeded with

N706NA, the first of two NASA U-2ERs (former ER-2s) used to survey the earth's resources; programs include water resource evaluation, land use development, disaster assessment, and stratospheric sampling. Lockheed

Designation	Serial Number	Comments
U-2ER-18	80-1063	NASA's Earth Resources air vehicle; NASA number N706NA; formerly designated ER-2
U-2RT-19	80-1064	Formerly designated TR-1B
U-2RT-20	80-1065	Formerly designated TR-1B
U-2R-21	80-1066	Formerly designated TR-1A
U-2R-22	80-1067	Formerly designated TR-1A
U-2R-23	80-1068	Formerly designated TR-1A
U-2R-24	80-1069	Formerly designated TR-1A
U-2R-25	80-1070	Formerly designated TR-1A
U-2R-26	80-1071	Formerly designated TR-1A
U-2R-27	80-1072	Formerly designated TR-1A
U-2R-28	80-1073	Formerly designated TR-1A
U-2R-29	80-1074	Formerly designated TR-1A
U-2R-30	80-1075	Formerly designated TR-1A
U-2R-31	80-1076	Formerly designated TR-1A
U-2R-32	80-1077	Formerly designated TR-1A
U-2R-33	80-1078	Formerly designated TR-1A
U-2R-34	80-1079	Formerly designated TR-1A
U-2R-35	80-1080	Formerly designated TR-1A
U-2R-36	80-1081	Formerly designated TR-1A
U-2R-37	80-1082	Formerly designated TR-1A
U-2R-38	80-1083	Formerly designated TR-1A
U-2R-39	80-1084	Formerly designated TR-1A
U-2R-40	80-1085	Formerly designated TR-1A
U-2R-41	80-1086	Formerly designated TR-1A
U-2R-42	80-1087	Formerly designated TR-1A
U-2R-43	80-1088	Formerly designated TR-1A

Another view of NASA U-2C (N708NA) prior to its retirement after eighteen years of service. Deployed air brake panels are noteworthy. NASA

Designation	Serial Number	Comments
U-2R-44	80-1089	Formerly designated TR-1A; delivered 3 October 1989
U-2ER-45	80-1090	NASA's number two Earth Resources air vehicle; NASA number N708NA; formerly designated ER-2

Note: Although somewhat different than earlier U-2Rs, recent U-2R (former TR-1) aircraft were designated as such simply to avoid confusion.

Chapter 13

A-12 Blackbird and D-21 Drone

The reason it carried Lockheed design number A-12 is because Kelly made twelve trips to Washington with design numbers A-1 through A-12 before the latter design was selected.

—*Rich Stadler*

The U-2 became operational on 30 June 1956. Simultaneously, U-2 program officials were predicting that its useful lifetime over the USSR would not last more than two years at the most. In fact, during its first mission over the USSR, its own onboard defense warning system verified that it not only had been detected by radar but had been tracked quite accurately throughout its overflight. Still it remained a key source for the gathering of intelligence information for forty-seven months—until 1 May 1960, when the U-2 being flown by Frank Powers was shot down near Sverdlovsk, Russia.

Project GUSTO

In the meantime, in an effort to reduce the radar cross section of the U-2, to make it harder to detect and track with radar, a high-priority program was undertaken to make the U-2 less vulnerable. New developments in radar-absorbing material were tried with successful results but not enough to completely solve the problem. In light of this, a number of strange designs for reconnaissance air vehicles were investigated. Most of these were optimized to operate at very high altitudes (100,000 feet plus) and relatively slow speed; they were balloon-type air vehicles with low-powered, long-duration powerplants. None of these proved practicable.

In the fall of 1957, Richard M. Bissell, director of the Central Intelligence Agency, began an investigative program to determine how far the probability of shooting down an aircraft varied respectively with its speed, altitude, and radar cross section. This analysis demonstrated that supersonic speed—the higher the better—would greatly reduce the aircraft's vulnerability to radar-guided surface-to-air missiles, the probability of being shot down was not reduced to zero, of course, but serious consideration was nonetheless undertaken. Thus, from the fall of 1957 onward, increased attention was focused on the creation of an air vehicle that could not only fly at high altitudes and high speeds, but employ the best radar-absorbing material available to it when it was ready.

The project to create such an advanced air vehicle was code named GUSTO, and the Skunk Works and the Convair Division of the General Dynamics Corporation were secretly informed of its general operational requirements.

Without government contracts and monies, both entities initiated preliminary and conceptual design work. Both firms' designers constantly refined their respective design parameters until late November 1958.

Of course, President Eisenhower and his scientific advisor, Dr. James Killian, knew about Project GUSTO. When Central Intelligence Agency officials informed them of their findings through Lockheed's Skunk Works and Convair, Ike gave his approval to proceed. Lockheed and Convair were simultaneously authorized to submit definitive proposals, the two companies were funded, and the U-2 follow-on program was officially launched.

Ten of the 15 A-12 OXCART aircraft parked on a ramp somewhere within the Nellis Air Force Base test ranges complex, circa 1963. The second aircraft from the bottom is the one-of-a-kind A-12T that was used for pilot check-outs and VIP rides. It was in this plane that A-12 designer Kelly Johnson was treated to a ride on 20 July 1963. Lockheed; Tony Landis

Both proposals were completed in July 1959, and on 20 July, President Eisenhower was again briefed. He gave his final go-ahead, and the high-priority program proceeded.

It became time to select the winning design. On 20 August 1959, specifications of the two proposals were submitted to a joint Central Intelligence Agency, Department of Defense, and U.S. Air Force source selection panel. The specifications of the two proposals were as follows:

Specifications	Lockheed	Convair
Maximum speed	Mach 3.2	Mach 3.2
Range (total)	4,120 nautical miles	4,000 nautical miles
Range (at altitude)	3,800 nautical miles	3,400 nautical miles
Cruise altitudes		
Start	84,500 feet	85,000 feet
Midrange	91,000 feet	88,000 feet
End	97,600 feet	94,000 feet
Dimensions		
Length	102 feet	79.5 feet
Wingspan	57 feet	56 feet
Other		
Gross weight	110,000 pounds	101,700 pounds
Fuel weight	64,600 pounds	62,000 pounds
First flight	22 months	22 months

Project OXCART

The Skunk Works' entry, designated A-11 in-house, was chosen. Project GUSTO was terminated, and the new program to develop a U-2 follow-on aircraft was code named OXCART.

On 3 September 1959, the Central Intelligence Agency authorized the Skunk Works to proceed with its antiradar studies, aerodynamic structural tests, and engineering designs. On 30 January 1960, the Skunk Works was given the official go-ahead to manufacture twelve A-11 aircraft.

Kelly Johnson and his preliminary design engineers had produced a series of Project GUSTO configurations running from A-1 through A-11, the last being the winner for Project OXCART. It was a large single-seat, twin-engine, twin-tail design with a long gooosenecklike forward fuselage and delta wings. It was to be manufactured of titanium alloy, and its two engines would be carried in midwing nacelles.

In the meantime, the Pratt & Whitney division of the United Aircraft Corporation had been involved in project discussions and had undertaken a program to develop the propulsion system for the aircraft. Its Model JT11 (J58) turbojet engine, which would ultimately propel the A-11, had been sponsored originally by the U.S. Navy for its own purposes. The Central Intelligence Agency contracted with Pratt & Whitney to further develop its J58—already rated Mach 3—to be optimized for a speed rating of Mach 3.2. A contract was let, calling for the initial assembly of three experimental XJ58 engines for durability and reliability tests and the provision of three service test YJ58 engines for flight testing of the first A-11, beginning in early 1961.

Johnson, creator of the U-2, was the chief designer of the A-11. Models of the A-11 were tested and retested, adjusted and readjusted during thousands of wind tunnel hours. Johnson was confident of his design, but no one could say with authority whether the bird

A fine study of the tenth A-12—Lockheed serial number 130, U.S. Air Force serial number 60-6933—which now survives at the San Diego Aerospace Museum. Lockheed; Tony Landis

would fly—still less whether it would meet the very demanding requirements laid down for it. Indeed, manned flight at triplesonic speed was possible for a short duration, but long-duration triplesonic speed was still unexplored.

To generate engineering drawings and test models in wind tunnels was one thing; to actually build the aircraft and successfully fly it was another. Most difficulties stemmed from the basic fact that in flying through the atmosphere at Mach 3.2, the skin of the aircraft would be subjected to temperatures of more than 550 degrees Fahrenheit—and for long periods of time. No current metal alloy commonly used in production aircraft would stand such temperatures, and alloys that would were too heavy for the most part, thus not suitable for the A-11's structure.

During the design phase, Skunk Works engineers looked at many metal alloys and finally selected a titanium alloy. Characterized by great strength and relatively light weight, it featured good resistance to high temperatures. Titanium was also scarce and very expensive, and methods for milling it and controlling the quality of it were not fully developed. Of the early deliveries from Titanium Metals Corporation, some 80 percent had to be rejected. It was not until 1961 that a delegation from OXCART headquarters visited the officials at that firm to inform them of the objectives and high priority of the OXCART program. Following the classified visit, Titanium Metals' full cooperation was gained, and their supply of titanium alloy to Lockheed became consistently satisfactory.

This only solved one early problem, however. One virtue of titanium is its extreme hardness, but this same quality gave rise to immense difficulties in machining and shaping the alloy. Drill bits that worked well on aluminum alloy quickly shattered; new drill bits for titanium had to be devised. Assembly line production was impossible, so each example of the small OXCART fleet was—so to speak—manufactured by hand. The cost of the program rose well above original estimates, and it quickly started to run behind schedule. One after another,

however, the problems were solved. Their solution constituted the greatest technological achievement of the entire project. From then on, it became practicable, albeit expensive, to build aircraft out of various titanium alloys.

Since every additional pound of weight was critical to the A-11, adequate insulation was out of the question. The inside of the aircraft would be like a moderately hot oven: 250 degrees Fahrenheit. The pilot would have to wear a kind of space suit, with its own cooling apparatus, pressure control, oxygen supply, and other necessities for survival. The aircraft's fuel tanks, which made up the greatest part of the vehicle, would heat up to about 350 degrees Fahrenheit, so a special fuel had to be developed, and the tanks themselves made inert with nitrogen gas. Lubricating oil was formulated for operation at 600 degrees Fahrenheit and contained a diluent in order to remain fluid at operation below 40 degrees Fahrenheit. Insulation on the plane's intricate wiring quickly became brittle and useless. During the lifetime of the OXCART program, no better insulation was found; the wiring and related connectors had to be given special attention and handling at great cost in labor and time.

The OXCART was to carry one highly sophisticated camera that was very delicate; it needed a special window made of quartz glass. This created another unique problem. The effectiveness of the whole system depended upon achieving complete freedom from optical distortion, despite the great heat to which the window would be subjected. Thus, the question was not simply one of providing equipment with resistance to high temperature, but one of ensuring that the temperature would be even throughout the area of the window. It took three years of time and $2 million to arrive at a satisfactory solution. The program scored one of its most remarkable successes when the quartz glass was successfully fused to its titanium alloy frame by an unprecedented process involving the use of high-frequency sound waves.

Another major problem of a very different nature was to achieve the low radar cross section desired. The airframe areas giving the greatest radar return were the vertical stabilizers, the engine air inlets, the sides of the fuselage, and the outboard forward sides of the engine nacelles. Research in ferrites, high-temperature—absorbing materials, and high-temperature plastic structures was undertaken to find methods to reduce the return of radar waves, Eventually, the vertical tails were constructed from a kind of laminated plastic material; it was the first time such a material had been employed for an important

part of an aircraft's structure. With such changes in its structure and structural materials, the A-11 was officially—but secretly—redesignated the A-12. This was not publicly disclosed until long after the Lockheed A-12 program was over.

To test the effectiveness of antiradar devices, a small-scale model is useless; only a full-size mockup will do. Accordingly, the Skunk Works built one of these and as early as November 1959, transported it in a specially designed truck trailer over hundreds of miles of highway from the Burbank plant to the classified test area. There it was hoisted to the top of a pylon to be "looked at" from various angles by radar. Tests and adjustments went on for a year and a half before the results were deemed satisfactory. In the course of the process, it was found desirable to attach some sizable metallic constructions on either side of the fuselage and on the outboard forward sides of the engine nacelles. Johnson understandably worried a great deal about the aerodynamic effect of the protuberances on his design. In flight testing, however, it later came about that they bestowed a useful aerodynamic lift to the air vehicle. Years later, Lockheed's design for a supersonic transport embodied similar structures.

OXCART Pilots

Obviously, OXCART pilots would have to be extraordinary in

Inflight view of A-12 number nine— Lockheed serial number 129, U.S. Air Force serial number 60-6932—in near all-black dress. Lockheed

their skills at flying and very competent—not only because of the unprecedented performance of the aircraft themselves, but also because of the particular qualities needed in individuals who were to fly the intelligence-gathering missions. Brigadier General Don Flickinger of the U.S. Air Force was designated to draw up the criteria for pilot selection, with advice from Kelly Johnson and from Central Intelligence Agency Headquarters. These pilots had to be qualified in the latest high-performance fighters, emotionally stable, and highly motivated. They were to be between twenty-five and forty years of age, and the size of the A-12 cockpit prescribed that they be under 6 feet tall and under 175 pounds in weight.

When the final screening was complete, the pilots chosen for the program were

Kenneth S. Collins
Ronald J. ("Jack") Layton
Francis J. Murray
Walter R. Ray
Russell Scott
William L. Skliar
Dennis B. Sullivan
Mele Vojvodich, Jr.
Lon Walter
Jack W. Weeks
David P. Young

After the selection of these original eleven A-12 pilots, arrangements were made with the U.S. Air Force to effect appropriate transfers and assignments to cover their training and to lay the basis for their transition from military to civilian status. Compensation and insurance arrangements were similar to those for the U-2 pilots.

Aircraft Basing and Testing

One thing to be decided in the earliest stages of the program was where to base and test the aircraft. Lockheed clearly could not do the business at its Burbank facility where the aircraft were being built, if for no other reason, because its runway was too short. The ideal location would be remote and away from populated areas; far away from civil and military airways to eliminate observation; easily accessible by air; blessed with good weather year-round; equipped with fuel storage facilities; fairly close to a U.S. Air Force installation; and in possession of at least an 8,000 foot runway. No such place existed.

Ten U.S. Air Force bases programmed for closure were considered, but none provided the required security, and the annual operating costs of most of them would be unacceptable. The North Base Area of Edwards Air Force Base seemed a more likely candidate, but in the end, it too was passed over. Instead, the secluded Groom Lake test site in Nevada was finally selected. It was lacking in personnel accommodations and fuel storage, and its long-unused runway was inadequate. But base security was good, or could be made so, and a moderate construction program could provide sufficient facilities.

Lockheed estimated what would be required with respect to monthly fuel consumption,

hangars and maintenance shops, personnel housing, and runway specifications. Loaded with a list of priority needs, Central Intelligence Agency Headquarters produced a plan for construction and engineering. Moreover, in case anyone grew curious about the activities at this remote site, a cover story stated that the facilities were being prepared for specific-but-not-named radar studies to be conducted by an engineering firm with U.S. Air Force support. The remote area was explained as necessary to lower the effect of electronic interference from outside sources.

Base construction began in earnest on 1 September 1960 and continued on a double-shift schedule until 1 June 1964. One urgent task was to build the runway, which, according to initial estimates of A-12 requirements, had to be at least 8,500 feet long. The existing asphalt runway was 5,000 feet long and not capable of supporting the weight of A-12 aircraft. The new runway was constructed between 7 September and 15 November 1960 and involved pouring over 25,000 yards of concrete. Another major problem was to provide some 500,000 gallons of PF-1 (JP-7) aircraft fuel each month. Neither fuel storage tanks nor a means of transporting fuel to them existed. After considering airlift, pipeline, and truck transportation, it was decided that truck was the most

Chapter Thirteen

economical. This was accomplished in part by resurfacing some 18 miles of highway leading into the base.

Three surplus U.S. Navy hangars were obtained, dismantled, and erected on the north side of the base. Over 100 surplus U.S. Navy housing buildings were transported to the base and made ready for occupancy. By early 1962, a fuel tank farm was ready, with a capacity of 1,320,000 gallons. Warehousing and shop space was begun, and repairs made to older buildings. All this, together with the many other facilities that had to be provided, took a long time to complete. But the essential facilities were ready in time for the forecast delivery date of the first A-12 in August 1961.

The essential facilities were ready; however, the A-12 was not. The promised date for first delivery, originally 31 May 1961, slipped to August, largely because of Lockheed's difficulties in obtaining and fabricating titanium alloy. Moreover, Pratt & Whitney found unexpectedly great trouble in bringing the J58 engine up to OXCART requirements. According to the unclassified Lockheed document *The OXCART Story* by Thomas P. McIninch, in March 1961, Kelly Johnson notified Central Intelligence Agency Headquarters: "Schedules are in jeopardy on two fronts. One is the assembly of the wing and the other

is in satisfactory development of the engine. Our evaluation shows that each of these programs is from three to four months behind the current schedule."

To this, Bissell replied: "I have learned of your expected additional delay in first flight from 30 August to 1 December 1961. This news is extremely shocking on top of our previous slippage from May to August and my understanding as of our meeting 19 December that the titanium extrusion problems were essentially overcome. I trust this is the last of such disappointments short of a severe earthquake in Burbank."

Realizing that delays were causing the cost of the program to soar, Central Intelligence Agency Headquarters decided to place a top-level aeronautical engineer in residence at the Skunk Works to monitor the program and submit progress reports.

Delays nevertheless persisted. On 11 September 1961, Pratt & Whitney informed Lockheed of its continuing difficulties with the J58 engine in terms of weight, delivery, and performance. The completion date for the first A-12 now had slipped to 22 December 1961, and the first flight to 27 February 1962. Even on this date, the J58 would not be ready, and it was therefore decided that the Pratt & Whitney J75 engine, developed for the Republic F-105 Thunderchief and flown in the U-2

Eye-level ground view of A-12MD number one—Lockheed serial number 134,
U.S. Air Force serial number 60-6940—
the 14th production A-12. The D-21's
tail fairing—a la the space shuttle
during 747 piggyback rides—is noteworthy. Lockheed; Tony Landis

and other aircraft, should be used
for early flights. The J75, along
with other components, could be
fitted to the A-12 airframe, and it
could power the aircraft safely to
altitudes up to 50,000 feet and at
speeds up to Mach 1.6.

When this decision had been
made, final preparations were
begun for the testing phase. In
December 1961, Colonel Robert J.
Holbury of the U.S. Air Force was
named commander of the secret
base, with a Central Intelligence
Agency employee as his deputy.
Support aircraft began arriving in
the spring of 1962. These included
eight McDonnell F-101 Voodoos for
training, two Lockheed T-33s for
proficiency flying, one Lockheed
C-130 Hercules for cargo
transportation, a U-8A for
administration purposes, a

helicopter for search and rescue,
and a Cessna 180 for liaison use.
Lockheed provided an F-104
Starfighter to act as chase aircraft
during the A-12 flight test period.

Meanwhile, in January 1962,
an agreement was reached with the
Federal Aviation Administration
that expanded the restricted
airspace in the vicinity of the test
area. Certain Federal Aviation
Administration air traffic
controllers were cleared for the
OXCART project; their function
was to ensure that aircraft did not
violate the order. The North
American Air Defense Command
established procedures to prevent
its radar stations from reporting
the appearance of high-
performance aircraft on their radar
scopes.

Refueling concepts required prepositioning of vast quantities of fuel at certain points outside the United States. Special tank farms were programmed in California and at Eielson Air Force Base, Alaska; Thule Air Base, Greenland; Kadena Air Base, Okinawa; and Adana, Turkey. Since the A-12 aircraft was to use specially refined fuel—JP-7—these tank farms were reserved exclusively for use by the OXCART program. Very small groups of technicians at these locations maintained the fuel storage facilities and arranged for periodic quality control fuel tests.

At Lockheed's Burbank plant, the first A-12, serial number 121, received its final systems tests and check-out during January and February 1962 and was partially disassembled for shipment to the site. Movement of the full-scale radar test model had been successfully accomplished in November 1959 (as discussed earlier in this chapter). A thorough survey of the route in June 1961 ascertained the hazards and

A-12MD number one being prepared for a developmental D-21 drone test; note the details of the cockpit wind screen and canopy. Lockheed; Tony Landis

problems of moving the actual aircraft and showed that a package measuring 35 feet wide and 105 feet long could be transported without major difficulty. Obstructing road signs had to be removed, trees trimmed, and some roadsides leveled. Appropriate arrangements were made with police authorities and local officials to accomplish the safe transport of the first and subsequent A-12 aircraft. The entire fuselage, minus wings, was crated, covered, and loaded on a specially designed trailer, which cost about $100,000. On 26 February 1962, the first A-12 departed Burbank, and arrived at the secret base according to plan.

First Flights

Upon the arrival of the A-12, reassembly of the aircraft and installation of two interim J75 engines began. Soon it was found that aircraft tank sealing compounds had failed to adhere to the metals, and when fuel was put into the tanks, numerous leaks occurred. It was necessary to strip the tanks of the faulty sealing compounds and reline them with new sealing materials. Thus occurred one more unexpected and exasperating delay in the program.

Finally, on 26 April 1962, the first A-12 was ready. On that day, in accordance with Kelly Johnson's custom, test pilot Louis ("Lou") Schalk of Lockheed took it for an "unofficial" and "unannounced" first flight lasting some 40 minutes. As in all first flights, minor problems were detected, but it took only four more days to ready the unique aircraft for its first "official" flight.

On 30 April 1962, just under one year later than originally planned, the number one A-12 officially lifted its wheels from the runway. Piloted again by Lou Schalk, it took off at 255 miles per hour, with a gross weight of 72,000 pounds, and climbed to 30,000 feet. Top speed was 510 miles per hour, and the flight lasted 59 minutes. Schalk reported that the aircraft responded well and was extremely stable. Johnson declared this to be the smoothest official first flight of an aircraft he had designed or tested.

The aircraft went supersonic on its second official flight, 4 May 1962, hitting Mach 1.1. Again, only minor problems were reported.

With these flights accomplished, jubilation was the order of the day. The new director of the Central Intelligence Agency, John McCone, sent a telegram of congratulations to Johnson. A critical phase had been triumphantly passed, but the long, difficult, and sometimes discouraging process of working the aircraft up to full operational performance remained.

The second A-12, number 122, arrived at the base on 26 June 1962 and spent three months in radar testing before engine installations and final assembly. Air vehicle three, A-12 number 123, arrived in August and flew in October. A two-seat version intended for use in training project pilots—air vehicle four, A-12 number 124—was delivered in November. It was to be the first example powered by the J58 engines, but delivery delays and a desire to begin pilot training prompted a decision to install the lower-thrust J75s. The trainer, nicknamed *Titanium Goose*, flew initially in January 1963. The fifth A-12, serial number 125, arrived at the site on 17 December 1963.

Meanwhile, the OXCART program received a boost from the Cuban Missile Crisis. U-2s had been maintaining a regular reconnaissance vigil over the island of Cuba, and it was on one of these missions in October 1962 that the presence of offensive missiles was discovered. Overflights thereafter became more frequent, but on 27 October local time, a Central Intelligence Agency U-2, flown by a Strategic Air Command pilot on a Strategic Air Command-directed mission, was shot down by a surface-to-air missile. This raised the dismaying possibility that continued manned, high-altitude surveillance of Cuba might become out of the question. The OXCART program suddenly assumed greater significance than ever, and its achievement of operational status became a high national priority.

At the end of 1962, two A-12 aircraft were engaged in flight test activities. A maximum speed of Mach 2.16 and altitude of 60,000 feet had been attained. Progress was still slow, however, because of delays in the delivery of engines and shortcomings in the performance of those delivered. The first A-12 was still flying with two J75 engines, and the second with one J75 and one J58. It had long since become clear that Pratt & Whitney had been optimistic in its forecast; the problem of developing the J58 up to OXCART specifications had proved a good deal more difficult than expected. According to McInich in *The OXCART Story*, John McCone judged the situation to be truly serious, and on 3 December 1962, he wrote to the president of United Aircraft Corporation: "I have been advised that J58 engine deliveries have been delayed again due to engine control production problems. By the end of the year it appears we will have barely enough J58 engines to support the flight-test program adequately. Furthermore, due to various engine difficulties we have not yet reached design speed and altitude. Engine thrust and fuel consumption deficiencies at present prevent sustained flight at design conditions which is so necessary to complete developments."

The first flight with two of J58

engines installed occurred on 15 January. By 31 January 1963, ten J58 engines were available. From then on, all A-12 aircraft were fitted or retrofitted with their intended propulsion system. Flight testing accelerated, and contractor personnel went to a three-shift workday.

With each succeeding step into a high-Mach-number regime, new problems presented themselves. The worst of all these difficulties—indeed one of the most formidable in the whole history of the program—was revealed when flight testing moved into speeds between Mach 2.4 and Mach 2.8, and the aircraft experienced such severe roughness as to make its operation virtually out of the question. The trouble was diagnosed as being in the engine air inlet system, which,

with its controls, admitted air into the J58 powerplants. At the higher speeds, the flow of air was uneven, and the engine therefore could not function properly. Only after a long period of experimentation, often highly frustrating and irritating, was a solution reached. This further delayed the day when the A-12 could be declared operational.

While on a routine flight on 24 May 1963, a Central Intelligence Agency pilot recognized an erroneous and confusing air speed indication and decided to eject from the aircraft, which crashed 14 miles south of Wendover, Utah. The pilot, Kenneth Collins, was unhurt. The wreckage was recovered from the impact area in two days, and persons on the scene were identified and requested to

Rare inflight view of A-12MD number one with a pylon-mounted GTD-21A drone riding piggyback. This airplane survived, and it is on permanent dis- *play inside the Museum of Flight in Seattle, Washington. Lockheed; Tony Landis*

sign secrecy agreements. A cover story for the media described the accident as occurring to an F-105 fighter, and it is still listed in this way on official records.

All A-12s were grounded for one week during investigation of the accident. A plugged pitot static tube in icing conditions turned out to be responsible for the faulty cockpit instrument indications. It was a minor problem that did not hold up progress for long.

The President's Announcement

In spite of the crash, and in spite of the editor of *Aviation Week* (as might be expected) indicating his knowledge of developments at Burbank, 1963 went by without any public revelation. President Lyndon Johnson was brought up-to-date on the project a week after taking office and directed that a paper be prepared for an announcement in the spring of 1964. At his press conference on 24 February, he read a statement, of which the first paragraph was as follows:

> The United States has successfully developed an advanced experimental jet aircraft, the A-11, which has been tested in sustained flight at more than 2,000 miles per hour and at altitudes in excess of 70,000 feet. The performance of the A-11 far exceeds that of any other aircraft in the world today. The development of this aircraft has been made possible by major advances in aircraft technology of great significance for both military and commercial

applications. Several A-11 aircraft are now being flight tested at Edwards Air Force Base in California. The existence of this program is being disclosed today to permit the orderly exploitation of this advance technology in our military and commercial program.

The president went on to mention the "mastery of metallurgy and fabrication of titanium metal" that had been achieved. He gave credit to Lockheed and to Pratt & Whitney, remarked that appropriate members of the Senate and House had been kept fully informed, and prescribed that the detailed performance of the A-11 would be kept strictly classified.

The president's reference to the A-11 was, of course, deliberate, as A-11 had been the original design designation for the all-metal aircraft first proposed by Lockheed; subsequently, it became the design designation for the U.S. Air Force YF-12A interceptor, which differed from its parent mainly in that it carried a second crew member for launching air-to-air missiles. To preserve the distinction between the A-11 (the YF-12A) and the A-12 (follow-on to the U-2), security had briefed practically all witting personnel in government and industry on the impending announcement. Project OXCART secrecy continued in effect. Speculation about a Central Intelligence Agency role in the A-11 development was considerable, but it was never acknowledged by the government. News headlines ranged from "United States Has a Dozen A-11 Jets Already Flying" to "Secret of Sizzling New Plane Probably History's Best Kept."

The president also said that examples of "the A-11 [YF-12A] now at Edwards Air Force Base are undergoing extensive tests to determine their capabilities as long-range interceptors." It was true that the U.S. Air Force had on 31 October 1960, contracted for three interceptor versions of the A-12, and they were by February 1964 available. But at the moment when President Johnson spoke, no YF-12As were at Edwards and none ever had been. Project officials had known that the public announcement was about to be made, but they had not been told exactly when. Caught by surprise, they hastily flew two U.S. Air Force YF-12As to Edwards from their secret base to support the president's statement. So rushed was this operation, so quickly were the aircraft put into hangars upon arrival, that the heat from the planes activated the hangar sprinkler system, dousing the reception team that awaited them.

Thenceforth, while the A-12 continued its secret career at its own site, the YF-12A performed at Edwards in the glare of the public. Pictures of the aircraft appeared in the press, correspondents could look at it and marvel, stories could be written. Virtually no details

were made available, but the technical journals nevertheless had a field day. The unclassified *Air Force and Space Digest*, for example, published a long article in its issue of April 1964, commencing: "The official pictures and statements tell very little about the A-11 [YF-12A]. But the technical literature from open sources, when carefully interpreted, tells a good deal about what it could and, more importantly, what it could not be. Here's the story. . . ."

Readiness for Operational Use

Three years and seven months after its first flight in April 1962, in November 1965, the A-12 was declared ready for operational use at design specifications. The period that had been devoted to flight test activities had been remarkably short, considering the new fields of aircraft performance that were being explored. As each higher Mach number was reached, exhaustive tests were carried out in accordance with standard procedures to ensure that the aircraft functioned properly and safely. Defects were corrected, and improvements made. All concerned gained experience with the particular characteristics and idiosyncrasies of the A-12 air vehicles.

The engine air inlet and related control system continued for a long time to present a troublesome and refractory problem. Numerous attempts failed to find a remedy, even though a special task force concentrated on the difficulties. For a time, something approaching despair accompanied the puzzle, and the solution, when finally achieved, was greeted with enormous relief. After all, not every experimental aircraft of highly advanced performance has survived its flight testing period. The possibility existed that OXCART also would fail, despite the great cost and effort expended upon it.

The main burden of test flights fell upon Lockheed test pilots, and some of the aircraft that became available at the site were reserved for the most advanced testing. At the same time, however, the detachment pilots were receiving training and familiarizing themselves with the new A-12. In the course of doing so, they contributed a good many ideas for improvements, and their own numerous flights shortened the time required for the test program as a whole. Indeed, one feature of OXCART development was this intimate collaboration between Lockheed, Lockheed test pilots, operational pilots, and Central Intelligence Agency officials, all of whom worked in concert with astounding effectiveness.

On 20 July 1963, the aircraft flew for the first time at Mach 3; in November 1963, Mach 3.2—the design speed—was reached at 78,000 feet altitude. By 31 December 1963, 573 flights had been made, totaling 765 hours. Nine aircraft were in the inventory. The longest sustained flight at design conditions came about on 3 February 1964; it lasted 10 minutes at Mach 3.2 and 83,000 feet. By 31 December 1964, 1,160 flights had been made, totaling 1,616 hours. Eleven aircraft were then available, four of them reserved for testing and seven assigned to the detachment.

The chronology of A-12 performance increases can be put in another way: Mach 2 was reached after six months of flying, Mach 3 after fifteen months. Two years after first flight, the aircraft had flown a total of 38 hours at Mach 2, 3 hours at Mach 2.6, and less than 1 hour at Mach 3. After three years, Mach 2 time had increased to 60 hours, Mach 2.6 time to 33 hours, and Mach 3 time to 9 hours; all Mach 3 time, however, was logged by test aircraft, and detachment aircraft were still restricted to Mach 2.9.

As may be seen from the preceding figures, most flights were of short duration, averaging little more than an hour each. Primarily, this was because longer flights were unnecessary at this stage of testing. It was also true, however, that the less seen of A-12s the better, and short flights helped to preserve the secrecy of the program. Yet, it was virtually

Right-side profile view of A-12MD number one during A-12–D-21 aerodynamic compatibility trials. Lockheed

impossible for an aircraft of such size and performance to remain inconspicuous. At its maximum speed, the A-12 had a turning radius of no less than 86 miles. It could in no way stay close to its test site; its shortest possible flights took it over a very large piece of the American Southwest.

The first long-range, high-speed flight came about on 27 January 1965, when one of the four test aircraft flew for 1 hour and 40 minutes, with 1 hour and 15 minutes above Mach 3.1; its total range was 3,870 miles, at altitudes between 75,600 and 80,000 feet.

Two more A-12s were lost during this phase of the program. On 9 July 1964, aircraft number 133 was making its final approach to the runway when, at an altitude

of 500 feet and an air speed of 350 miles per hour, it began a smooth, steady roll to the left. Test pilot William M. ("Bill") Park of Lockheed could not overcome the roll. At about 45-degrees of bank angle and 200 feet of altitude, he ejected. As he swung down to the vertical in the parachute, his feet touched the ground, for a narrow escape in the perilous history of test piloting. The main cause of the accident was later determined to be that the servo for the right outboard roll and pitch control froze. No news of the accident filtered out.

On 28 December 1965, aircraft number 126 crashed immediately after takeoff and was totally destroyed. Detachment pilot Mele Vojvodich ejected safely at an

After taking over Senior Bowl operations, a Boeing B-52H Stratofortress *carries two underwing GTD-21B drones. Lockheed*

altitude of 150 feet. The accident investigation board determined that a flight line electrician had improperly connected the yaw and pitch gyros—had in effect reversed the controls; again, no publicity was connected with the accident. To stop such mistakes in the future, the wiring was color coded.

The year 1965 saw the test site reach the high point of activity. Completion of construction brought it to full physical size. All detachment pilots were Mach 3 qualified. Site population reached 1,835. Contractors were working three shifts a day. Lockheed Constellation aircraft made daily flights between the factory at Burbank and the site. Two C-47 flights a day were made between the site and Las Vegas, where program personnel lived. And

A-12 officials were planning how and when and where to use OXCART in its appointed reconnaissance role.

OXCART Targeting

After the end of U-2 flights over the USSR, United States political authorities were understandably cautious about committing themselves to further manned reconnaissance over unfriendly territory. No serious intention existed to use the A-12 over Russia and its republics; except in some unforeseeable emergency, it was indeed no longer necessary to do so. What, then, should be done with this airplane?

The first interest was the island nation of Cuba just off the Florida coast. By early 1964, Project OXCART Headquarters began planning for the contingency of flights over Cuba under a program code named Skylark. Bill Park's accident in early July held this program up for a time, but on 5 August 1964, it was ordered that Skylark achieve emergency operational readiness by 5 November. This involved preparing a small detachment that would do the job over Cuba, though at something less than the full design capability of the A-12s. The goal was to operate at Mach 2.8 and 80,000 feet altitude.

The OXCART aircraft, however, were never used over Cuba. U-2s proved adequate, and the A-12 was kept for more critical situations.

In 1965, a more critical situation did indeed emerge in Asia, and interest in using the A-12 aircraft there began to increase. On 18 March, John McCone discussed with Cyrus R. Vance and Secretary of Defense Robert S. McNamara the increasing hazards to U-2 aircraft and drone reconnaissance of Communist China. According to *The OXCART Story* by Thomas P. McInich, a memorandum of those talks stated:

> It was further agreed that we should proceed immediately with all preparatory steps necessary to operate the OXCART over Communist China, flying out of Okinawa. It was agreed that we should proceed with all construction and related arrangements. However, this decision did not authorize the deployment of the OXCART to Okinawa nor the

decision to fly the OXCART over Communist China. The decision would authorize all preparatory steps and the expenditure of such funds as might be involved. No decision has been taken to fly the OXCART operationally over Communist China. This decision can only be made by the President.

Four days later, Brigadier General Jack C. Ledford of the U.S. Air Force, director of the Office of Special Activities at the Pentagon, briefed Vance on the scheme that had been drawn up for operations in the Far East. The project was called Black Shield, and it called for the A-12s to operate out of Kadena Air Force Base. In the first phase, three A-12s would stage to Okinawa for sixty-day periods, twice a year, with about 225 personnel involved. After this was in good order, Black Shield would advance to the point of maintaining a permanent detachment at Kadena Air Force Base. Secretary Vance made $3.7 million available to be spent in providing support facilities on the island, which were to be ready by early fall 1965.

Meanwhile, the North Vietnamese began to deploy radar-guided surface-to-air missiles around Hanoi, thereby threatening military reconnaissance capabilities. Secretary McNamara called this to the attention of the undersecretary of the U.S. Air Force on 3 June 1965 and inquired about the practicability of substituting A-12s for U-2s. He was told that Black Shield could operate over Vietnam as soon as adequate aircraft performance was achieved.

With deployment overseas thus apparently impending for the fall of 1965, the detachment went into the final stages of its program for validating the reliability of the A-12s and their systems. It set out to demonstrate complete aircraft systems reliability at Mach 3.05 and at a range of 2,300 nautical miles, at a 76,000 feet penetration altitude. A demonstrated capability for three aerial refuelings was also part of the validation process.

By this time, the A-12 was well along in performance. The engine air inlet, camera, hydraulic, navigation, and flight control systems all demonstrated acceptable reliability. Nevertheless, as longer flights were conducted at high speeds and high temperatures, new problems surfaced, the most serious being with the electrical wiring system. Wiring connectors and components had to withstand temperatures of more than 800 degrees Fahrenheit, together with structural flexing, vibration, and shock. Continuing malfunctions in the engine air inlet controls, communications equipment, electronic countermeasures systems, and cockpit instruments were in many cases attributable to wiring failures. Also, disturbing evidence indicated that careless ground crew handling was contributing to electrical connector failures. Difficulties persisted in the sealing of fuel tanks. What with one thing and another, officials soon began to fear that the scheduled date for Black Shield readiness would not be met. Prompt corrective action on the part of the Skunk Works was in order. The quality of maintenance needed drastic improvement. The responsibility for delivering a whole aircraft system with acceptable reliability to meet an operational commitment lay entirely within Lockheed's hands.

In this uncomfortable situation, John Parangosky, deputy for technology, Office of Special Activities, went to Lockheed to see Kelly Johnson on 3 August 1965. A frank discussion ensued on the measures necessary to ensure that Black Shield commitments would be met, and Johnson concluded that he should himself work full-time at the site in order to get the job done expeditiously. President Daniel Haughton of Lockheed offered the full support of the corporation, and Johnson began duty at the site the next day. His firm and effective management got Black Shield back on schedule.

Four primary A-12 aircraft were selected for final validation, and flights were conducted. During these tests, the A-12 achieved a maximum speed of Mach 3.29, a maximum altitude of 90,000 feet, and a sustained flight time above

Mach 3.2 of 1 hour and 14 minutes. The maximum endurance flight lasted 6 hours and 20 minutes. The last stage was reached on 20 November 1965, and according to McInich's *The OXCART Story* two days later, Johnson wrote Brigadier General Jack Ledford: "Over-all, my considered opinion is that the aircraft can be successfully deployed for the Black Shield mission with what I would consider to be at least as low a degree of risk as in the early U-2 deployment days. Actually, considering our performance level of more than four times the U-2 speed and three miles more operating altitude, it is probably much less risky than our first U-2 deployment. I think the time has come when the bird should leave its nest."

Meanwhile, flight testing and crew proficiency training continued at the site. An impressive demonstration of the A-12's capability came about on 21 December 1966, when test pilot Bill Park of the Skunk Works— who made his first flight in an A-12 on 23 November 1963— flew 10,198 statute miles in 6 hours. The airplane left the Nevada test area and flew northward over Yellowstone National Park, then eastward to Bismarck, North Dakota, and on to Duluth, Minnesota. Park then turned south and passed Atlanta, Georgia, en route to Tampa Bay, Florida, then northwest to Portland, Oregon, and

then southwest to Nellis Air Force Base, Nevada. Park's flight established an aviation record— albeit an untold one due to security—unapproachable by any other aircraft in the world, including the North American XB-70 Valkyrie, which, after 129 flights between two prototypes, produced a best of Mach 3.07, 74,000 feet, and much shorter distances flown. Park's flight began at about the same time a typical government employee starts a workday, and ended 2 hours before quitting time.

Shortly after Park's historic flight, tragedy struck Project OXCART. During a routine training flight on 5 January 1967, A-12 number four was lost, together with its pilot. The mishap occurred during descent about 70 miles from home base. A fuel gauge failed to function properly, and the aircraft ran out of fuel only minutes before landing. The pilot, Walter Ray—who made his first A-12 flight on 10 February 1963— ejected but was killed when he failed to separate from the ejection seat prior to impact. The plane's wreckage was found the next day, and Ray's body was recovered a day later. Through U.S. Air Force channels, a story was released to the effect that a U.S. Air Force SR-71, on a routine test flight out of Edwards Air Force Base, was missing and presumed down in Nevada. (This cover story was used because the A-12 was still

175

secret.) The pilot was identified as a civilian test pilot, and the newspapers connected him with Lockheed. Flight activity at home base was again suspended during investigation of the causes both for the crash and for the failure of the seat separation device.

None of the four A-12 accidents occurred in the high–Mach number, high-temperature regime of flight. All mishaps involved traditional problems inherent in any airplane. In fact, the A-12 was by this time performing at high speeds, with excellent reliability.

Operation Black Shield

About May 1967, prospects for A-12 deployment took a new turn. A good deal of concern was evident in Washington, D.C., about the possibility that the Communists might introduce surface-to-surface missiles into North Vietnam, and concern was aggravated by doubts as to whether the United States could detect such a development if it occurred. President Johnson asked for a proposal on the matter; the Central Intelligence Agency suggested that the OXCART be used. Its camera was far superior to those on drones or on the U-2; its vulnerability was far less. The state and defense members of the committee decided to reexamine the requirements and the political risks involved. While they were engaged in their deliberations, Director of Central Intelligence

Richard Helms submitted to the 303 Committee another formal proposal to deploy the OXCART. In addition, he raised the matter at President Johnson's Tuesday lunch on 16 May and received the president's approval to "go." Walt Rostow, later in the day, formally conveyed the president's decision, and the Black Shield deployment plan was forthwith put into effect.

On 17 May 1967, the airlift to Kadena Air Force Base began. On 22 May, the first A-12 flew nonstop to Kadena in 6 hours and 6 minutes. A second A-12, U.S. Air Force serial number 60-6930, departed home base on 24 May and arrived at Kadena 5 hours and 55 minutes later. The third A-12, U.S. Air Force serial number 60-6932, left according to plan on 26 May and proceeded normally until in the area of Wake Island, where the pilot experienced difficulties with the inertial navigation and communications systems. Under these circumstances, he decided to make a precautionary landing at Wake Island. The prepositioned emergency recovery team secured the aircraft without incident, and the flight to Kadena resumed the next day.

On 29 May 1967, the unit at Kadena was ready to fly its first operational mission. Under the command of Colonel Hugh C. Slater of the U.S. Air Force, who made his first A-12 flight on 30 June 1965, 260 personnel had

Test pilot Louis ("Lou") Schalk of the Skunk Works was the first to fly the number one a-12 air vehicle, officially on 30 April 1962; the unofficial first flight occurred on 26 April. Lockheed

deployed to the Black Shield facility at Kadena Air Force Base. Except for hangars, which were a month short of being completed, everything was in place for sustained OXCART operations. On 30 May, the detachment was alerted for mission number one on 31 May, and the moment arrived that would see the culmination of ten years of effort, worry, and cost. As fate would have it, on the morning of the thirty-first, heavy rain fell at Kadena. Since weather over the target area was clear, preparations continued in hopes that the local weather would clear. When the time for takeoff approached, the OXCART, which had never operated in heavy rain, taxied to the runway, and took off while the heavy downpour continued.

The first Black Shield mission followed one flight line over North Vietnam and one over the demilitarized zone. It lasted 3 hours and 39 minutes, and the cruise legs were flown at Mach 3.1 and 80,000 feet. Results were satisfactory. Seventy of the 190 known surface-to-air missile sites in North Vietnam were photographed, as were nine other priority targets. No radar signals were detected, indicating that the first mission had gone completely unnoticed by both the Chinese and the North Vietnamese.

Fifteen Black Shield missions were alerted between 31 May and 15 August 1967. Seven were flown,

and of these, four detected radar tracking signals, but no hostile action was taken against any of them.

A typical Black Shield mission over North Vietnam included an aerial refueling shortly after takeoff, south of Okinawa, the planned photographic pass or passes, withdrawal to a second aerial refueling in the Thailand area, and return to Kadena. So great was the A-12's speed that it spent only 12.5 minutes over North Vietnam in a typical *single-pass* mission, or a total of 21.5 minutes on two passes. Its 86 mile turning radius at this speed, however, forced the aircraft to fly into Chinese airspace at times.

Between 16 August and 31 December 1967, twenty-six missions were alerted. Fifteen were flown. On 17 September, one surface-to-air missile site tracked the A-12 with its acquisition radar but was unsuccessful with its Fan Song guidance radar. On 28 October, a North Vietnamese surface-to-air missile site for the first time launched a single, albeit unsuccessful, missile at the OXCART. Photography from this mission documented the event with pictures of missile smoke above the surface-to-air missile firing site and of the missile and its contrail. The A-12's electronic countermeasures equipment appeared to perform well against the missile's guidance radar.

During the flight of 30 October 1967, A-12 pilot Dennis Sullivan, who made his first A-12 flight on 14 April 1965, detected radar tracking on his outbound pass over North Vietnam. Two missile sites prepared to launch surface-to-air missiles, but neither followed through. During his inbound pass, at least six missiles were fired at his A-12, each confirmed by missile vapor trails on mission photography. Sullivan saw these vapor trails and witnessed three missile detonations. Postflight inspection of the OXCART revealed that a piece of metal had penetrated the lower right-hand wing fillet area and lodged against the support structure of the wing tank. The fragment was not a warhead pellet but may have been a part of the debris from one of the missile detonations observed by Sullivan.

Between 1 January and 31 March 1968, six missions were flown out of fifteen alerted. Four of these were over North Vietnam, and two over North Korea. The first mission over North Korea on 26 January occurred during a very tense period following seizure of the United States Ship (USS) *Pueblo* on the twenty-third. The aim was to discover whether the North Koreans were preparing any large-scale hostile move on the heels of the incident. Chinese tracking of the flight was apparent, but no surface-to-air missiles were fired at the A-12.

Between 1 April and 9 June 1968, two missions were alerted for North Korea, but only one mission, on 8 May, was authorized. After this, no further OXCART missions were granted approval, for the improved SR-71 had become operational and would soon replace the less capable A-12.

Project SENIOR BOWL

During the course of OXCART development, two A-12s—Lockheed build numbers 134 and 135, U.S. Air Force serial numbers 60-6940 and 60-6941—were modified to carry and launch Lockheed D-21 remotely piloted reconnaissance drones under Project SENIOR BOWL. These air vehicles required a two-person crew in which the second crew member, sitting behind the pilot, would launch and direct the drone's flight. The A-12MD (*MD* meaning Missile Director) planes never flew operational missions, however, because of one serious mishap during developmental testing of the system.

On 3 July 1966, A-12MD number two was lost during a D-21 drone-launch test off Point Mugu, near Oxnard, California. Test pilot Bill Park of the Skunk Works flew the OXCART to optimum speed (over Mach 3) and altitude (some 92,500 feet) for a test launch. Reconnaissance system operator Ray Torick of the Skunk Works, who made his first A-12 flight on 17 June 1965, then launched the

GTD-21 drone. Instead of the drone flying off and away from the A-12 on a clean separation, it collided with the aft end of the A-12, breaking the aircraft in half. Park ejected safely and survived the ordeal. Torick survived the ejection, but before he was rescued his pressure suit filled with water and he was drowned.

Other D-21 developmental flight test evaluations proved unworthy of high-altitude, high-speed launches; as a result, modified GTD-21Bs were launched subsonically from B-52H bombers of the 4200th Test Wing at Beale Air Force Base. After the demise of the SENIOR BOWL program, the unused D-21 drones were moth-balled at Davis-Monthan Air Force Base.

Summary of the OXCART Program

The OXCART program lasted just over ten years, from its inception in 1957 through its first flights in 1962 to its termination in 1968. Lockheed's Skunk Works produced fifteen A-12s. Six A-12s were lost in accidents; two pilots were killed, and two pilots had narrow escapes. In addition, two F-101 Voodoo chase planes were lost with their U.S. Air Force pilots during OXCART's test phases.

The main objective of the program—to create a dedicated reconnaissance air vehicle of unprecedented speed, range, and altitude capability—was triumphantly achieved. It may well be, however, that the most important aspects of the effort lay in its by-products: the notable advances in aerodynamic design, engine performance, cameras, electronic countermeasures systems, pilot life-support systems, radar-avoidance devices, and above all else, the milling, machining, shaping, and welding of titanium alloy. Altogether, especially for Kelly Johnson and his Skunk Works workers, it was truly a pioneering accomplishment.

In a ceremony at Nellis Air Force Base's main base on 26 June 1968, Vice-Admiral Rufus L. Taylor, deputy director of Central Intelligence, presented the Central Intelligence Agency Intelligence Star for valor to pilots Kenneth S. Collins, Ronald J. Layton, Francis J. Murray, Dennis B. Sullivan, and Mele Vojvodich for their participation in Operation Black Shield. The posthumous award to pilot Jack W. Weeks (lost in an A-12 on a flight out of Okinawa on 5 June 1968) was accepted by his widow. The U.S. Air Force Legion of Merit was presented to Colonel Hugh C. Slater and his deputy, Colonel Maynard N. Amundson. The U.S. Air Force Outstanding Unit Award was presented to the members of the OXCART detachment—1129th Special Activities Squadron, Detachment 1—and the U.S. Air Force supporting units.

Wives of A-12 pilots were present and learned for the first time of the activities in which their husbands had been involved. Kelly Johnson was a guest speaker at the ceremony and lamented in moving words the end of an enterprise that had marked his most outstanding achievement in aircraft design. His own awards had already been received: the President's Medal of Freedom in 1964, and on 10 February 1966, the National Medal of Science, from President Johnson, for his contributions to aerospace science and to the national security of the United States of America.

A-12 Specifications

Type	Single-seat and tandem-seat, twin-engine, high-altitude, high-speed, long-range strategic reconnaissance, intelligence-gathering, and drone-launch aircraft
Wingspan	55 feet, 7 inches
Wing area	1,605 square feet
Length	98 feet, 9 inches
Height	18 feet, 3 inches
Empty weight	60,000 pounds
Maximum weight	120,000 pounds
Maximum speed	Mach 3.35
Service ceiling	95,000 feet
Rate of climb	Classified
Maximum range	2,500 miles (without inflight refueling)
Armament	None
Powerplant	2 afterburning Pratt & Whitney J58 turbojet engines

D-21 Specifications

Type	Unmanned, remote-piloted, high-altitude, high-speed, long-range reconnaissance missile drone
Wingspan	19 feet
Wing area	Classified
Length	43 feet, 2 inches
Height	Classified
Empty weight	Classified
Maximum weight	20,000 pounds (estimated)
Maximum speed	Mach 4 plus (estimated)
Service ceiling	100,000 feet plus (estimated)
Rate of climb	Classified
Maximum range	2,500 miles (estimated)
Armament	None

Powerplant   1 Marquardt RJ43-MA-11 ramjet engine

Note: D-21s were originally designated GTD-21As; then, after modifications for B-52H launching, they were redesignated GTD-21Bs.

A-12 Production

Designation	Lockheed Build Number	Serial Number	Comments
A-12	121	60-6924	Displayed at Blackbird Airpark, Palmdale, California
A-12	122	60-6925	Displayed at USS *Intrepid* Museum, New York
A-12	123	60-6926	Lost in crash in Nevada
A-12T	124	60-6927	Displayed at Los Angeles Museum, Los Angeles, California
A-12	125	60-6928	Lost in crash in Nevada
A-12	126	60-6929	Lost in crash in Nevada
A-12	127	60-6930	Located in Huntsville, Alabama
A-12	128	60-6931	Displayed at Minnesota Air National Guard Museum, Minneapolis-St. Paul International Airport, Minnesota
A-12	129	60-6932	Lost in crash off Midway Island on 5 June 1968
A-12	130	60-6933	Displayed at San Diego Aerospace Museum, San Diego, California
A-12	131	60-6937	In storage at Palmdale, California
A-12	132	60-6938	Displayed at USS *Alabama* Museum
A-12	133	60-6939	Lost in crash at Kadena Air Force Base, Okinawa
A-12MD	134	60-6940	Displayed at Museum of Flight, Seattle, Washington
A-12MD	135	60-6941	Lost in crash off Pt. Mugu, Oxnard, California, on 3 July 1966

Note: Lockheed A-12 build numbers range from 121 to 135, and six A-12s were lost; thus, nine survived.

D-21 Production

Note: Lockheed D-21 build numbers range from 501 to 539, and twenty-one D-21s were used; thus, seventeen were not.

Chapter 14

YF-12 Blackbird

Listen—you'll never learn anything by talking. The measure of an intelligent person is the ability to change his mind.

—Kelly Johnson

At 2:00 P.M. on 23 September 1959, the U.S. Air Force announced it had canceled Weapon System 202A, its proposed long-range interceptor experimental aircraft, the North American XF-108 Rapier. The F-108, projected to fly long distances at triplesonic cruise speed above 70,000 feet to intercept enemy bomber aircraft, was to be armed with three Hughes AIM-47A Falcon infrared-guided (heat-seeking) air-to-air missiles. As an all-weather interceptor, the F-108 was to incorporate the Hughes pulse-Doppler AN/ASG-18 radar and missile fire control system. The twin-engine Rapier was to be powered by two 30,000 pound-thrust-class General Electric J93 afterburning turbojet engines and was to supplement and ultimately replace the U.S. Air Force's Convair F-106 Delta Dart. The first F-108 example was to make its first test

flight in March 1961. When the F-108 program was terminated, only a full-scale engineering mockup had been completed; no production F-108 was under construction.

This unexpected and abrupt cancellation, as explained by the U.S. Air Force, occurred because of a shortage of funds and other priorities in U.S. Air Force programming. No technical difficulties were involved with the F-108, and all program objectives had been met. The U.S. Air Force said it would continue, "at a reduced level," the development of the Hughes AN/ASG-18 radar and fire control system and the Hughes AIM-47A Falcon missile, which was under development for the proposed U.S. Air Force Aerospace Defense Command F-108 Rapier. But history now reveals far more to this surprising cancellation than first realized.

YF-12 Development

As development of the A-12 under Project OXCART proceeded through the year 1959, Kelly Johnson realized the potential of creating derivative mission aircraft from the basic A-12 airframe and powerplant combination—one type being a highly advanced long-range, high-altitude, triplesonic-cruise, all-weather interceptor operated by a crew of two—that would outperform the U.S. Air Force's proposed F-108. Thus, with

Right-side profile view of YF-12A number one, circa 1963. First flown on 7 August 1963, this example logged 180.9 flight hours during 145 flights prior to its crash landing at Edwards Air Force Base; the rear half was used to build the SR-71C, which was later leased to NASA. Lockheed

A YF-12A during armament testing, circa 1964. The YF-12A carried three AIM-47 Falcon missiles, but production F-12Bs would have carried four. Lockheed; Tony Landis

the blessing of Lockheed management, Johnson was authorized to design an improved manned interceptor version of the OXCART for U.S. Air Force scrutiny. After design, Lockheed offered it to the U.S. Air Force as a dedicated air defense interceptor.

This version of the A-12 was discussed with Brigadier General Howell M. Estes, Jr., of the U.S. Air Force—who finally got a ride in an SR-71 on 5 November 1987—in Washington, D.C., on 16 and 17 March 1960. General Estes and Dr. Courtlandt Perkins, U.S. Air Force secretary for research and development, were impressed with Lockheed's interceptor proposal, and Johnson was directed to have further discussions with General Marvin Demler at Wright-Patterson Air Force Base. Again, Lockheed's proposed interceptor was well received.

In mid-1960, Lockheed's Skunk Works was authorized to build three service test long-range

The large, 40 inch diameter of the AN/ ASG-18 radar antenna and an infrared sensor ball, or eyeball. The circular- *cross-section fuselage and raised cockpit canopies are noteworthy. Lockheed; Tony Landis*

interceptors based on the A-12's airframe. The proposed long-range air defense fighter was called the improved manned interceptor, and the Skunk Works was directed to use the aforementioned Hughes radar, fire control, infrared sensor, and missile armament systems on the airplane. The interceptor trio, which were built alongside the A-12s, were not given an official designation at the time because of the type's top-secret classification.

Only after the triservice action on 18 September 1962 to redesignate aircraft in an effort to stop high-digit numbers and interservice designation confusion

did the improved manned interceptor receive its YF-12A designation. Without the Defense Department's redesignation program, the Lockheed YF-12A might have received the designation YF-112A, because the General Dynamics F-111 was already on order.

In any event, working closely with Hughes, Johnson's team of Skunk Works engineers and assembly workers modeled and produced the first YF-12A in just under three years. In July 1963, it was trucked from Palmdale to the secret Groom Lake test facility within Nellis Air Force Base. In

A YF-12A and one of its three air-to-air AIM-47A Falcon missiles. Note the ab- *sence of infrared sensor balls. Lock-heed; Tony Landis*

the hands of test pilot James D. ("Jim") Eastham of the Skunk Works, it made a successful first flight on 7 August. The second YF-12A made its first flight on 26 November 1963; it was flown by test pilot Lou Schalk of the Skunk Works, who had made the first flight of the A-12. The third YF-12A, piloted by the Skunk Works' Robert J. ("Bob") Gilliland, made its first flight on 13 March 1964. Suddenly, without fanfare, the U.S. Air Force had a fighter-interceptor that was incomparable to any other on earth. And no one except those in the know were aware of its existence.

Knowing about the YF-12A's matchless capabilities, U.S. Air Force officials requested its procurement and production to ultimately replace the so-called ultimate interceptor: the F-106. The U.S. Air Force wanted to purchase at least ninety-three examples, to be designated F-12B.

New defense secretary Robert McNamara and his "whiz kids," however, saw it another way, even though Congress had voted three times in three years to appropriate

Worm's-eye, head-on view of a YF-12A at Edwards Air Force Base, circa 1964. Lockheed

Overhead view of YF-12A number three, which was flown 198 times, totaling 449.8 flight hours, prior to its loss in a crash at Edwards Air Force Base on 24 June 1971; this aircraft was used during the YF-12's speed and altitude record flights in May 1965. Lockheed

$90 million to start production of the F-12B for the U.S. Air Force Aerospace Defense Command. Each time, McNamara froze these monies, opting instead to fund the less expensive and adequate F-106X proposal from the Convair division of General Dynamics. Finally, it too was rejected.

During development of the F-12 as a missioned weapons system, it took three years finally to track a target and launch at it a heat-seeking AIM-47A missile. The main problem was being able to open a missile bay door, eject a missile downward, and fire it so that it would fly straight and true rather than penetrate the air vehicle between the pilot's and fire control officer's cockpits. In reality, even at much lower speeds, serious problems plagued aircraft missile launchings. But at a Mach number over 3 at very high altitude, no one had ever fired a missile. Once again, Lockheed's Skunk Works had to slice through new air.

To keep the missiles away from the YF-12A, Skunk Works engineers had to develop onboard thruster units, one above each end of a missile in each missile bay, to push each missile downward with equal force—all in a few seconds. After a missile had been ejected downward some 40 feet below the aircraft, it would ignite.

Four Hughes Aircraft engineers, working as fire control officers, fired AIM-47As at a number of target drones at altitudes ranging from sea level to more than 100,000 feet, and hit targets more than 140 miles distant over ocean or over land. Fired from the YF-12A at Mach 3 plus, and accelerating on its own, an AIM-47A sped hypersonically at Mach 7 at the peak of its flight profile.

The AN/ASG-18 radar system and AIM-47A missile performed fantastically after the launch problem was eliminated. As a result, the success rate was over 90 percent. Development of the missile in the YF-12A program led to the successful development of the Hughes radar, fire control system, and missile used in today's Grumman F-14 Tomcat.

Unfortunately, instead of equipping the U.S. Air Force Aerospace Defense Command with F-12B aircraft, a decision was made to downgrade its role. That action also doomed further production of F-106 interceptors, as only 340 examples (277 single-seat, 63 tandem-seat) were ultimately produced—less than that of any other contemporary U.S. Air Force fighter aircraft.

Worse, McNamara's team viewed the existence of tooling for the F-12B as a threat to funding for the B-70 and the F-15. Without an F-12B production contract in hand, the Skunk Works kept its tooling for several years after cancellation. Then, for a mere $0.075 per pound, Lockheed was ordered to scrap all tooling for the proposed F-12B. At

YF-12A number two in NASA dress climbs to begin one of its NASA missions flown between 1969 and 1978. Beneath the belly of the airplane is a heat transfer unit, which exposed experiments to rapid temperature rises during sustained flight at high supersonic speeds. This YF-12A was retired to the U.S. Air Force Museum on 7 November 1979 after 279 total flights and 534.7 flight hours. NASA

the time, according to Johnson, each F-12B would have cost about $19 million. And even today, at any cost for a fully missioned fighter-interceptor, no airplane in existence—either at home or abroad—performs like the F-12.

At the time of the YF-12A program demise, the three service test examples made a total of 640 Lockheed, Air Force, and NASA flights. The one-of-a-kind YF-12C, created from an SR-71A, U.S. Air Force serial number 64-17951, was flown eighty-nine times by Lockheed, Air Force, and NASA pilots; it carried serial number 60-6937 to avoid confusion with the fleet of SR-71As but was counted among the total of thirty-two SR-71As built.

YF-12A Records
On 1 May 1965, YF-12A number three was used to establish three world records:
1. A straight course speed of 2,070.101 miles per hour at an absolute sustained altitude of 80,257.65 feet. The airplane was flown by Colonel Robert L. Stephens, and Lieutenant Colonel Daniel Andre acted as fire control officer.
2. A closed course speed of 1,688.889 miles per hour. The airplane was flown by Lieutenant Colonel Walter F. Daniel, and Major James P. Cooney was fire control officer.
3. A 500 kilometer closed course speed of 1,643.041 miles per hour. The air vehicle was flown by Lieutenant Colonel Walter F. Daniel, and Major Noel T. Warner was fire control officer.

As a dedicated air defense weapons system, with unmatched performance characteristics, the YF-12A proved to be one fantastic airplane. Through no fault of its designers, developers, and producers, however, it simply was overtaken by the technological advances it helped create. But soon, its successor—the SR-71—bore the best fruit on the Blackbird family tree.

YF-12 Specifications

Type	Tandem-seat, twin-engine, high-altitude, high-speed, long-range, all-missile-armed interceptor
Wingspan	55 feet, 7 inches
Wing area	1,605 square feet
Length	105 feet, 2.5 inches
Height	18 feet, 3 inches
Empty weight	60,730 pounds
Maximum weight	127,000 pounds
Maximum speed	Mach 3.35
Service ceiling	85,000 feet
Rate of climb	Classified
Maximum range	2,250 miles (without inflight refueling)

Test pilot James D. ("Jim") Eastham of the Skunk Works was the first to fly the number one YF-12A on 7 August 1963. He is shown here just before boarding a YF-12A *for yet another flight test. Note the pressure suit and air conditioning unit. Lockheed; Tony Landis*

| Armament | 4 infrared-guided (heat-seeking) Hughes AIM-47A long-range air intercept missiles |
| Powerplant | 2 afterburning Pratt & Whitney J58 turbojet engines |

YF-12 Production

Designation	Serial Number	Comments
YF-12A-00-LO	60-6934	Damaged in crash; rebuilt as SR-71C 64-17981
YF-12A-00-LO	60-6935	Displayed at the U.S. Air Force Museum, Wright-Patterson Air Force Base, Dayton, Ohio
YF-12A-00-LO	60-6936	Lost in crash on 24 June 1971

Note: Lockheed YF-12 build numbers range from 1001 to 1003, and one YF-12 was lost and one YF-12 was used to create the SR-71C; thus, one survived.

Good in-flight view of YF-12A number one before it was painted black; black paint was suggested by Ben Rich to help reduce heat at high Mach numbers. Lockheed

Landing gear retracts as YF-12A-1 lifts off on yet another test hop out of Edwards Air Force Base after it was painted black. USAF; James Goodall Collection; Tony Landis

YF-12A number two, one of three YF-12As assigned to a high-speed research program at NASA's Ames/Dryden Flight Research Facility at Edwards Air Force Base, begins to climb on one of its many research programs flown between 1969 and 1978. These programs comprised 297 U.S. Air Force–NASA–Lockheed flights flown by two YF-12As and the one-of-a-kind YF-12C. Beneath the belly of the aircraft is a heat transfer unit that exposed experiments to rapid temperature rises during sustained supersonic flights of Mach 1 through Mach 3. NASA

SR-71 Blackbird

The use of dual vertical tails canted inward on the engine nacelles took advantage of the chine vortex in such a way that the directional stability improves as the angle of attack of the aircraft increases.

—*Kelly Johnson*

The U.S. Air Force had been extremely supportive of A-12 operations all through the OXCART program. It assisted financially, conducted aerial refuelings, provided operational facilities at Kadena, and provided transportation to OXCART personnel and supplies to Okinawa for operations over North Vietnam and North Korea. It also ordered a small fleet of A-12s under Project Senior Crown: six air vehicles, which upon their completion as tandem-seat reconnaissance aircraft would be designated SR-71s. As originally planned, these would become operational around the year 1967.

The stated mission of the SR-71 was to conduct poststrike reconnaissance—that is, to look the enemy situation over after a nuclear exchange. Using the aircraft in this capacity hardly appeared likely, but the proposed

SR-71 was also to be capable of ordinary intelligence-gathering missions. For these purposes, though, the A-12 possessed certain clear advantages. It carried only one person, and largely for this reason, it had room for a much bigger and better camera as well as for various other collection devices that at the time could not be carried by the SR-71. It was certainly the most effective reconnaissance aircraft on earth, or likely to be in existence for years to come. Moreover, the A-12 was operated by civilians— Central Intelligence Agency pilots—and could be flown covertly, or at least without the number of personnel and the amount of fanfare normally attending a U.S. Air Force operation.

The order for six SR-71s, however, eased the course of OXCART development, because it meant that the financial burden was now shared even more with the U.S. Air Force. In addition, the cost of each air vehicle was somewhat reduced by the production of larger numbers. In the longer run, though, the existence of the SR-71 spelled the doom of the A-12, for reasons that appear to have been chiefly financial.

Demise of the A-12

During November 1965, when OXCART was finally declared operational, moves toward the demise of the A-12 commenced. Within the Bureau of the Budget, a memorandum was circulated expressing concern at the costs of the A-12 and SR-71 programs—past, current, and projected. It questioned the requirement for the total number of aircraft represented in the combined fleets and doubted the necessity for a separate Central Intelligence Agency fleet of A-12s. Several alternatives were proposed to achieve a substantial reduction in the forecasted spending, but the recommended course of action was to phase out the A-12 program by September 1966 and stop any further procurement of SR-71 aircraft beyond the half dozen already ordered. Copies of the memorandum were sent to the Department of Defense and the Central Intelligence Agency with the suggestion that those agencies explore the set of alternatives

spelled out in the paper. But the secretary of defense, Robert McNamara, declined to consider the proposal, presumably because the SR-71 would not be operational by September 1966, after which he would leave that government position.

Things remained status quo until July 1966, when the Bureau of the Budget proposed that a study group be established to look into the possibility of reducing expenses on both the OXCART and Senior Crown programs. The group was requested to consider the following alternatives:
1. Retention of separate, similar A-12 and SR-71 fleets
2. Collocation of the two fleets
3. Transfer of the A-12 mission and aircraft to the U.S. Air Force Strategic Air Command
4. Transfer of the A-12 mission to the Strategic Air Command and stowage of the A-12 fleet
5. Transfer of the A-12 mission to the Strategic Air Command and disposal of the A-12 fleet

The study group included C. W. Fischer, Bureau of the Budget; Herbert Bennington, Department of Defense; and John Parangosky, Central Intelligence Agency. This group conducted its study through the fall of 1966 and identified three principal alternatives of its own:
1. Maintain the status quo and continue both fleets at current approval levels.
2. Moth-ball all A-12 aircraft, but

Three SR-71A Blackbirds in various stages of production at Lockheed's Site 2 facility, U.S. Air Force Plant 42, Palmdale. Lockheed

maintain the OXCART capability by sharing SR-71 aircraft between SAC and the CIA.

3. Terminate the A-12 fleet in January 1968—assuming that an operational readiness date of September 1967 for the SR-71 had been met—and assign all missions to the SR-71 fleet.

On 12 December 1966, a meeting at the Bureau of the Budget was attended by Richard Helms, George Schultze, Cyrus Vance, and Dr. Hornig, scientific advisor to President Lyndon Johnson. Those present voted on the alternatives proposed in the Fischer-Bennington-Parangosky paper. Vance, Schultze, and Hornig chose to terminate the OXCART fleet, and Helms stood out for eventual sharing of the SR-71 fleet between the Central Intelligence Agency and Strategic Air Command. The Bureau of the Budget immediately prepared a letter to President Johnson setting forth the course of action recommended by the majority. Helms, having dissented from the majority, requested his deputy director for science and technology to prepare a letter to the president stating the Central Intelligence Agency's reasons for remaining in the reconnaissance business.

On 16 December 1966, Schultze handed Helms a draft memorandum to President Johnson that requested a decision either to share the SR-71 fleet

Rare inflight photograph of SR-71A
number one during one of its many
flights prior to its loss in a crash on 11

April 1969 following a takeoff accident.
Lockheed

Robert J. ("Bob") Gilliland made the
first flight of SR-71A number one
on 22 December 1964 at Groom Lake.
Lockheed

between the Central Intelligence
Agency and the Strategic Air
Command or to terminate the
Central Intelligence Agency
capability entirely. This time,
Helms replied that new
information of considerable
significance had been brought to
his attention concerning SR-71
performance. He requested another
meeting after 1 January 1967 to
review pertinent facts and also
asked that the memorandum to the
president be withheld pending that
meeting's outcome. Specifically, he
cited indications that the SR-71
program was having serious
technical problems (these remain
classified and therefore cannot be
discussed here) and that it was not
likely to achieve an operational
capability by the time suggested
for termination of the A-12
program, in January 1968. Helms

Eleven of the 31 SR-71s produced together at Beale Air Force Base, California. Lockheed

therefore changed his position from a bid for sharing the SR-71 aircraft with Strategic Air Command to a firm recommendation for retaining the OXCART A-12 fleet under Central Intelligence Agency sponsorship—period. The Bureau of the Budget's memorandum was nevertheless transmitted to the president, who, on 28 December 1966, accepted the recommendations of Vance, Schultze, and Hornig and directed the termination of the OXCART program by 1 January 1968.

First Flights and Deliveries of the SR-71

On 22 December 1964, with pilot Robert Gilliland of the Lockheed SR-71 project at the controls, the first SR-71A was successfully flight-tested for the first time at Groom Lake. About one year later, on 18 November 1965, the SR-71B trainer version made its first flight. Development on the SR-71 continued ahead of schedule, despite Richard Helms' warning of technical difficulties within the Senior Crown program. On 10 May 1966, the 9th Strategic Reconnaissance Wing at Beale Air Force Base accepted its first operational SR-71A. Deliveries of SR-71 aircraft continued, and in fact, the original order for six aircraft had been increased to thirty-one aircraft over several subsequent years.

Meanwhile, President Johnson's decision to terminate the OXCART program by 1 January 1968 meant that a schedule had to be formed for an orderly phaseout

Overhead view of the twelfth SR-71A, U.S. Air Force serial number 64-17961. Imagine the leading edges of the wings running straight to the engine nacelles and the circular part of the fuselage, *and you will see what the original A-11 OXCART looked like; the redesign to add chines resulted in the final OXCART configuration, the A-12. Lockheed*

SR-71A number six flies formation with
a U-2R to show very different designs
for the same mission. Lockheed

of the A-12 fleet. After consultation
with OXCART Project
Headquarters, the deputy secretary
of defense was advised on 10
January 1967 that four A-12s would
be placed in storage in July 1967,
two more by December, and the
last three by 31 January 1968. In
May 1967, Cyrus Vance directed
that the SR-71 assume contingency
responsibility to conduct Cuban
overflights as of 1 July 1967 and
take over the dual capability above
Southeast Asia and Cuba by 1
December 1967. This provided for
some overlap between OXCART
withdrawal and SR-71 assumption
of responsibility.

Until 1 July 1967, the OXCART
detachment was to maintain its
capability to conduct operational

missions both from a prepared
location overseas and from the
United States. This included a
fifteen-day quick reaction
capability for deployment to the
Far East and a seven-day quick
reaction for deployment over Cuba.
Between 1 July and 31 December
1967, the A-12 fleet would remain
able to conduct operational
missions either from a prepared
overseas base or from home base,
but not from both simultaneously.
A quick deployment time for either
Cuban overflights or deployment
to Southeast Asia would likewise
be maintained through this time
period.

All these transactions and
arrangements occurred before the
OXCART had conducted a single

An SR-71A hooked up to a KC-135
Stratotanker from behind and below.
NASA

The 15th SR-71A shows off its lines.
Lockheed

operational mission or even deployed to Kadena for such a mission. In the months after the aircraft first performed its appointed role over North Vietnam on 31 May 1967 local time, it demonstrated both its exceptional technical capabilities and the competence with which its operations were managed. As word began to get around that the A-12s would be phased out, high government officials began to voice their disquiet. Concern was shown by Walt Rostow, the president's special assistant; key congressional figures; members of the president's Foreign Intelligence Advisory Board; and the president's Scientific Advisory Committee. The phaseout slowed,

and the question of its advisability was reopened.

A new study of the feasibility and cost of continuing the OXCART program was completed in the spring of 1968, and four new alternatives were proposed:
1. Transfer all A-12 aircraft to Strategic Air Command by 31 October 1968, substitute the U.S. Air Force for contractor support where possible, and turn the test A-12 aircraft over to the SR-71 test facility.
2. Transfer A-12s as in alternative number one, and store eight SR-71s.
3. Close the A-12 home base and collocate the fleet of SR-71s at Beale Air Force Base, but with the Central Intelligence Agency

Head-on view of an SR-71A illustrates why many UFO sightings occurred during the career of the A-12–YF-12–

SR-71 series of Blackbird aircraft. Even today, the Blackbird looks out of this world. Tony Landis

retaining control and management. 4. Continue A-12 operations at the A-12's own base under Central Intelligence Agency control and management.

Richard Helms expressed his reactions to these alternatives in a memorandum to Nitze, Flax, and Hornig on 18 April 1968. In it, he questioned why, if eight SR-71s could be stored in one option, they could not be stored in all options, with the resultant savings applied in each case. He questioned the lower cost figures of combining the A-12s with the SR-71s and disagreed, for security reasons, with collocating the two fleets. Above all, however, he felt that the key point was the desirability of retaining a covert reconnaissance capability under Central Intelligence Agency (civilian) management. It was his judgment that such a requirement existed, and he recommended that the A-12s continue operations at home base under Central Intelligence Agency management.

In spite of all these belated efforts, Defense Secretary Clark M. Clifford reaffirmed the original decision to terminate the OXCART program and store the aircraft on 16 May 1968. At his weekly luncheon with his principle advisors on 21 May 1968, President Johnson confirmed Secretary Clifford's decision.

Early in March 1968, U.S. Air Force Strategic Air Command SR-71s began to arrive at Kadena to take over the Black Shield commitment, and by gradual stages, the A-12 was placed on standby to back up the SR-71. The last operational mission flown by an A-12 was on 8 May 1968 over North Korea, after which, the Kadena OXCART detachment was advised to prepare to go home. Project headquarters chose 8 June 1968 as the earliest possible date to begin redeployment, and in the meantime, flights of A-12s were to be limited to those essential for maintaining flying safety and pilot proficiency. After Black Shield A-12s arrived in the United States, they would be placed in storage. Those already at home base were placed in storage by 7 June 1968.

During the final days overseas, the A-12 program suffered yet another blow, as inexplicable as it was tragic. On 5 June 1968, air vehicle number 129, A-12 number nine, piloted by Jack Weeks, set out from Kadena on a check flight because of an engine change. Weeks was heard from when 520 miles east of Manila, near Midway Island. Then he disappeared. Search and rescue operations found nothing. No cause for the accident was ever ascertained. Once again, the official news release identified the lost aircraft as an SR-71, and security was maintained. The loss of A-12 number nine remains a mystery.

A few days afterwards, the two remaining A-12s on Okinawa flew to the United States and were stowed with the seven A-12s already in storage; thus, nine survived.

Project Senior Crown

With the end of OXCART A-12 activities, Senior Crown SR-71

operations blossomed fully. These would have been impossible, however, if not for Lockheed's Skunk Works and its marvelous array of engineers, then headed by Kelly Johnson. Even in the early

One of two SR-71Bs, U.S. Air Force serial number 64-17956, during its 1,000th sortie. Lockheed

The SR-71's best friend is an airborne tanker aircraft such as the Boeing KC-135, shown, and the McDonnell Douglas KC-10. Lockheed

An SR-71A immediately after liftoff at Palmdale. Note the Skunk Works logo on the tail. Tony Landis

1990s, the A-12, YF-12, and SR-71 Blackbird series of aircraft were still technological standouts. Practically every area of design required new approaches or breakthroughs in aviation-related technologies. For example, to withstand temperatures of more than 600 degrees Fahrenheit in the upper atmosphere during flight at more than three times the speed of sound, Blackbird planes required an array of specially developed materials including high-temperature fuel, sealants, lubricants, wiring, and other components.

Ninety-three percent of the Blackbird's airframe consisted of a titanium alloy that allowed the aircraft to operate in a regime where temperatures ranged from 450 degrees Fahrenheit at its aft midsection to 950 degrees Fahrenheit near the engine exhaust nozzles. The cockpit canopy, made of special heat-resistance glass, had to withstand surface temperatures as high as 640 degrees Fahrenheit.

Two Pratt & Whitney J58 turbojet engines with afterburner sections, each producing more than 34,000 pounds of maximum thrust, were housed in wing nacelles with diameters larger than that of the fuselage itself. Virtually every part of the complex engines had to be fabricated from special materials to meet the demands of triplesonic-plus speed. A translating (movable) spike in each engine air inlet controlled airflow, retracting aftward at speeds above Mach 1.6 to capture more air for the engines.

Suspension of SR-71 Operations

On 1 October 1989, all SR-71 operations—except for minimal

The one-of-a-kind SR-71A dubbed Big Tail. *The reason for the tail extension* *has not been made public. Lockheed;* Tony Landis

crew proficiency sorties—were suspended while the U.S. Air Force awaited the budget outcome for fiscal year 1990. With no new monies being voted for continued SR-71 activities, all U.S. Air Force SR-71 operations were terminated on 22 November 1989.

After entering service with the U.S. Air Force in early 1966, and following twenty-four years of duty with the Strategic Air Command, the Lockheed SR-71 was officially retired at Beale Air Force Base on 26 January 1990.

During their U.S. Air Force Strategic Air Command tenure, SR-71s flew a total of 53,490 flight hours, 17,300 missions, 3,551 operational missions, 11,008 operational hours, and 11,675 hours at Mach 3 plus and received 25,862 aerial refuelings.

Lieutenant Colonel Joseph T. Vida, SR-71 reconnaissance system operator for the U.S. Air Force, who made his first flight on 18

June 1975, achieved the high time in the SR-71 program on 6 March 1990 with a total of 1,392.7 flight hours; Colonel Robert M. Powell, SR-71 pilot for the U.S. Air Force, who made his first flight on 5 July 1967, achieved the high time as pilot with a total of 1,020.3 flight hours and got two Distinguished Flying Crosses.

On 6 March 1990, SR-71A 64-17972 was delivered to the Smithsonian Institution for permanent display at Dulles International Airport, Washington, D.C. En route, flying at normal operating speeds, this SR-71A— the same aircraft that had set the 1974 records—set four more world records, which included a Los Angeles, California, to Washington, D.C., time of 64 minutes and 2 seconds at an average speed of 2,144.8 miles per hour.

It was decided to donate the other nineteen surviving SR-71s to various museums and air bases for

Lieutenant Colonel Edward Yeilding, right, pilot, and Lieutenant Colonel Joseph T. Vida, reconnaissance systems operator (who has the highest time in SR-71s), pose in front of the SR-71A they set coast-to-coast and city-to-city world speed records in on 6 March 1990; Vida accumulated 1,392.7 hours of flying time in Blackbirds. Lockheed

public display while keeping six—three for Lockheed's Skunk Works, three for NASA—for future high-speed, high-altitude flight test programs.

SR-71s Loaned to NASA

Three SR-71 Blackbird aircraft have been loaned to NASA by the U.S. Air Force as testbeds for high-speed, high-altitude aeronautical research. The aircraft—an SR-71B (the only two-seat pilot trainer in operation) and two SR-71As—are based at NASA's Ames-Dryden Flight Research Facility at Edwards Air Force Base. They

have been assigned the following NASA numbers: NASA 831 (the one SR-71B), U.S. Air Force 64-17956, was manufactured in September 1965; NASA 832 (one SR-71A), U.S. Air Force 64-17971, was manufactured in October 1966; and NASA 844 (the other SR-71A), U.S. Air Force 64-17980, was built in July 1967. Respectively, when these aircraft were retired from the U.S. Air Force, their total times in flying hours were 3,760, 3,512.5, and 2,255.6.

Data from the SR-71 high-speed research program will be

The original A-12, left, and an SR-71A at Blackbird Airpark on its dedication ceremony day. A Pratt & Whitney J58 engine is displayed between them. Lockheed; Denny Lombard

used to aid designers of future supersonic and hypersonic aircraft and propulsion systems. Beneficiaries of this data include a future high-speed civil transport and the National Aero-Space Plane program.

The SR-71's operating environment makes it an excellent platform to carry out research and experiments in a variety of areas: aerodynamics, propulsion, structures, thermal protection materials, high-speed and high-temperature instrumentation, and sonic boom characterization. The SR-71 program at NASA's Ames-Dryden Flight Research Facility is part of NASA's overall high-speed aeronautical research program. It is expected to involve many NASA research centers and other government agencies.

In 1992, the SR-71 program manager at NASA's Ames-Dryden Flight Research Facility was David P. Lux. Each NASA SR-71 crew consisted of a pilot and a flight test engineer. Stephen D. Ishmael and Rogers E. Smith were assigned as SR-71 project pilots; Robert E. Meyer and Marta Bohn-Meyer, husband and wife, were assigned as SR-71 flight test engineers. Both pilot-engineer crews trained for many hours in the SR-71 flight simulator to become thoroughly acquainted with aircraft systems and operational procedures. The simulator was the same unit used by U.S. Air Force personnel at Beale Air Force Base before the

SR-71s were retired from military service in early 1990.

Flyable Storage

Lockheed's Skunk Works retains at Palmdale a trio of SR-71A aircraft that are operational and ready for experimental development flight test applications. These are SR-71As 64-17962, 64-17967, and 64-17968. Lockheed claims the airframes are good beyond the year 2020. It also points out that the SR-71 was excellent payload bay capabilities for up to 2,770 pounds of test instrumentation or other equipment, and that the aircraft can be readily modified to carry external items either above or below its fuselage.

Although the ultimate Blackbird is now retired from U.S. Air Force duties, and its many contributions to national security will never be fully revealed to the public, the SR-71 flies on with NASA and other government entities.

On 26 April 1992, a thirtieth anniversary celebration of the Blackbird's first flight—albeit based on the unofficial first flight date—was held at Blackbird Airpark in Palmdale. It was a fitting tribute to the exclusive club that has been associated with this unprecedented aircraft for more than a quarter of a century. It may well be another twenty-five years before the last Blackbird touches down on terra firma to stay. One can only wonder who will be present at Blackbird Airpark for the Blackbird's sixtieth anniversary celebration on 26 April 2022. . . .

SR-71 Records and Accomplishments

Date	Record or Accomplishment
26 April 1971	SR-71A completes 15,000 mile nonstop flight in 10 hours and 30 minutes with aerial refueling. The crew, Majors Thomas B. Estes and Dewain C. Vick, both of the U.S. Air Force, are awarded the 1971 Harmon and Mackey trophies for the flight.
1 September 1974	SR-71A sets New York, New York, to London, England, world speed record in 1 hour, 55 minutes, and 42 seconds. The crew is Majors James V. Sullivan and Noel Widdifield, both of the U.S. Air Force.
13 September 1974	SR-71A sets London, England, to Los Angeles, California, world speed record in 3 hours, 47 minutes, and 39 seconds. The crew is Captain Harold B. Adams and Major William C. Machorek, both of the U.S. Air Force.
27 July 1976	SR-71A sets world absolute and class records for speed over a 1,000 kilometer closed circuit at 2,092.294 miles per hour. The crew is Majors Adolphus H. Bledsoe, Jr., and John T. Fuller, both of the U.S. Air Force.
28 July 1976	SR-71A sets world absolute and class records for sustained altitude in horizontal flight at 85,069 feet. The crew is Captain Robert C. Helt and Major Larry A. Elliot, both of the U.S. Air Force.
28 July 1976	SR-71A sets world absolute and class records for speed at 2,193 miles per hour over a 15 kilometer-by-25 kilometer course. The crew is Captain Eldon W. Joersz and Major George T. Morgan, Jr., both of the U.S. Air Force.
6 March 1990	SR-71A sets four world records for speed: • Coast to coast in 67 minutes and 54 seconds at 2,124.5 miles per hour • Los Angeles, California, to Washington, D.C., in 64 minutes and 2 seconds at 2,144.8 miles per hour • Kansas City Kansas, to Washington, D.C., in 25 minutes and 59 seconds at 2,176.1 miles per hour • St. Louis, Missouri, to Cincinnati, Ohio, in 8 minutes and 32 seconds at 2,189.9 miles per hour The crew is Colonels Edward Yielding and Joseph T. Vida, both of the U.S. Air Force.

SR-71 Specifications

Type	Tandem-seat, twin-engine, high-altitude, high-speed, long-range strategic reconnaissance and intelligence-gathering aircraft
Wingspan	55 feet, 6 inches
Wing area	1,605 square feet
Length	107 feet, 4 inches
Height	18 feet, 5 inches
Empty weight	67,500 pounds
Maximum weight	172,000 pounds
Maximum speed	Mach 3.35
Service ceiling	92,500 feet
Rate of climb	Classified
Maximum range	3,250 miles (without inflight refueling)
Armament	None
Powerplant	2 afterburning Pratt & Whitney J58 turbojet engines

SR-71 Production

Note: Lockheed SR-71 build numbers range from 2000 to 2031; twelve SR-71s were lost between 10 January 1964 and 20 July 1972; thus, twenty survived.

NASA's SR-71B begins to retract its landing gear after takeoff from the main runway at Edwards Air Force Base; J58 engines were designed to operate in continuous afterburner. NASA

SR-71A Production

Designation	Serial Number	Comments
SR-71A	64-17950	Crashed 11 April 1967
SR-71A	64-17951	Redesignated YF-12C and given serial number 60-6937; displayed at Pima Air Museum, Tucson, Arizona
SR-71A	64-17952	Crashed 25 January 1966
SR-71A	64-17953	Crashed 10 January 1967
SR-71A	64-17954	Crashed 9 February 1966
SR-71A	64-17955	Displayed at Edwards Air Force Base, California
SR-71A(B)	64-17956	Converted to two-seat SR-71B; transferred to NASA Ames-Dryden Flight Research Facility, Edwards Air Force Base, California
SR-71A(B)	64-17957	Converted to two-seat SR-71B; crashed 12 January 1968
SR-71A	64-17958	Displayed at Warner Robbins Air Force Base, Georgia
SR-71A	64-17959	Displayed at Eglin Air Force Base, Florida
SR-71A	64-17960	Displayed at Castle Air Force Base, California
SR-71A	64-17961	Displayed at Beale Air Force Base, California
SR-71A	64-17962	In flyable storage at Palmdale, California
SR-71A	64-17963	Displayed at Beale Air Force Base, California
SR-71A	64-17964	Displayed at Offutt Air Force Base, Nebraska
SR-71A	64-17965	Crashed 25 October 1967
SR-71A	64-17966	Crashed 13 April 1967
SR-71A	64-17967	In flyable storage at Palmdale, California
SR-71A	64-17968	In flyable storage at Palmdale, California
SR-71A	64-17969	Crashed 10 May 1970 in Southeast Asia
SR-71A	64-17970	Crashed 17 June 1970 near El Paso, Texas
SR-71A	64-17971	Transferred to NASA Ames-Dryden Flight Research Facility, Edwards Air Force Base, California
SR-71A	64-17972	Used for trans-Atlantic and transcontinental speed record flights; displayed at Dulles International Airport, Washington, D.C.
SR-71A	64-17973	Displayed at Palmdale, California
SR-71A	64-17974	Crashed 21 May 1989 in South China Sea
SR-71A	64-17975	Displayed at March Air Force Base, California
SR-71A	64-17976	Displayed at U.S. Air Force Museum, Wright-Patterson Air Force Base, Dayton, Ohio
SR-71A	64-17977	Crashed, date unknown
SR-71A	64-17978	Crashed May 1973
SR-71A	64-17979	Displayed at Lackland Air Force Base, Texas

Featuring a maximum afterburning uninstalled thrust at sea-level static condition (standard day) of 34,000 pounds, the A-12, YF-12, and SR-71 aircraft powerplant is classified as a bleed bypass turbojet engine with an 8.8:1 pressure ratio. These engines, designated JT11D-20 by Pratt & Whitney and J58 by the U.S. Air Force, are designed for continuous operation in maximum afterburner; military thrust is about 85 percent of maximum afterburning thrust at sea level and some 55 percent at high altitude.

An SR-71A zooms past with both of its J58s in full afterburner, producing a combined thrust of about 68,000 pounds. Tony Landis

NASA's SR-71B, one of the three SR-71s lent to NASA by the U.S. Air Force, cruises over the Tehachapi Mountains on a flight from the NASA Ames/Dryden Flight Research Facility on Edwards Air Force Base. NASA's trio of Blackbirds—two SR-71As and the SR-71B—are used in high-speed, high-altitude research ventures in such areas as aerodynamics, propulsion, structures, thermal protection materials, and instrumentation. Data from the SR-71 research program could aid designers of future supersonic and hypersonic air vehicle and propulsion systems that could include a future high-speed civil transport and the National Aero-Space Plane. NASA

Designation	Serial Number	Comments
SR-71A	64-17980	Transferred to NASA Ames-Dryden Flight Research Facility, Edwards Air Force Base, California
SR-71A(C)	64-17981	Hybrid SR-71C aircraft created from salvaged parts, with rear half of YF-12A number one, 60-6934, and forward half of SR-71A functional engineering mockup; in long-term storage at Beale Air Force Base, California, as parts source

Note: Four SR-71As, 64-17982 through 64-17985, were canceled; a total of thirty SR-71As and one SR-71B were new-build aircraft. The SR-71C was a hybrid.

Chapter 16

XST

To design it [Have Blue], we took Maxwell's set of equations and reversed them to design an air vehicle with two-dimensional surfaces. This "facetting," allowed for the creation of a three-dimensional air vehicle with a series of flat panels rather than rounded surfaces. Today's computers like the Cray work faster which allowed us to design the F-22 in three dimensions from the outset. The result was—it doesn't require flat surfaces to achieve its stealth characteristics.

—*Ben Rich*

In the early 1970s, Russia developed and deployed advanced early warning radar networks, improved radar-guided surface-to-air missiles, and better fighter-interceptor planes with lookdown–shoot-down radar systems. The new and advanced air defense systems presented a significant threat to conventional United States aircraft. This threat was demonstrated clearly during the last years of the Vietnam War, and once again in the Middle East conflict of 1973. Worse, Russia's new threat could not be defeated by conventional electronics countermeasures equipment nor by current military tactics. Therefore, a solution to Russia's growing threat had to be devised, developed, and implemented. It had to be an unconventional cure.

Simultaneously, concurrent technological breakthroughs in *low-observable*, or *stealth*, technology for aircraft applications were coming to the forefront. These included the following:
- Advanced composite materials for internal and external airframe and powerplant structures to reduce substantially an aircraft's radar cross section
- Improved tactical weapons and advanced weapons delivery systems
- Improved radar-absorbing material and application processes of these special paint and putty materials to mask an aircraft's exterior protuberances such as rivet heads and gaps between access panels and equipment doors
- Improved measurement devices

that allowed engineers to measure radar cross section accurately so they could reduce an aircraft's radar cross section—by as much as 85 percent—by way of external shaping alone
- Advanced computer-generated aircraft design processes to speed development time and reduce cost
- Advanced fly-by-wire electronic flight control systems to replace basic aerodynamics lost to inherently unstable air vehicles about all three axes: pitch, roll, and yaw

These discoveries, in part, made it possible to counter the Russian threat in an unconventional manner: with a low-observable, or stealth, aircraft.

In late 1974, using the concurrent stealth technology discoveries, Lockheed's Skunk Works reinvented the airplane. With a new design idea called *faceting*, whereby angular surfaces on an aircraft's exterior are employed to deflect radar beams— much as the light beam from a flashlight deflects off an angled-

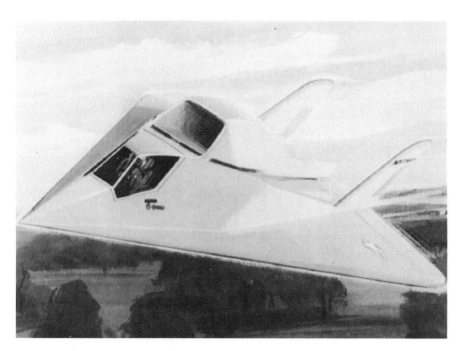

The proposed Northrop XST air vehicle used a combination of rounded and angular surfaces to achieve its lowered radar cross section. Other than this artist concept, little else has been released on Northrop's XST design, which lost the pole fly-off to Lockheed's XST design. Northrop

away flat surface—Skunk Works engineers designed a low-observable airplane configuration that countered all prior aircraft designs. Bill Schroeder, a Skunk Works aircraft designer, realized that he could best control radar cross section by using flat, faceted surfaces rather than conventional curved ones. Using faceting, his design appeared anything but aerodynamic. Denys Overholser, a pioneer Skunk Works software engineer, wrote a program that could compute the radar cross section of Schroeder's angular and jutted design.

The result of Schroeder's design and Overholser's computerization proved promising enough to proceed. With faceting, however, an obvious aerodynamic penalty surfaced: The airplane would be inherently unstable about all three axes—*pitch* (longitudinal stability), *roll* (lateral stability), and *yaw* (directional stability).

Although it had become clear to Lockheed that a multifaceted aircraft would present a highly reduced radar cross section to enemy radar networks, it was not immediately known how to make

Two views of Lockheed's XST air vehicle illustrate its unique configuration, which reduced the radar cross section *by as much as 85 percent by shaping alone.* Department of Defense

an unstable aircraft perform well in the air—and stability is a key requirement for accurately dropping bombs. Yet, Lockheed was convinced that it could develop and produce a viable stealth aircraft that would be stable and that would be difficult to detect and destroy using current and projected radar networks, radar-guided and heat-seeking ground-to-air and air-to-air missiles, and fighter aircraft with lookdown–shoot-down radar systems.

To actually create a viable stealth aircraft—specifically, an in-weather (nighttime) strike fighter—low-observable technology had to be demonstrated and validated by a manned experimental survivable testbed (XST) air vehicle. To do this in total secrecy, a highly classified program code-named Have Blue was initiated in the mid-1970s. Only personnel with the "need to know" about the top-secret program received clearances.

In early 1975, Lockheed and Northrop—and maybe other airframe contractors as well—received study contracts to (1) design an XST air vehicle and (2) produce a model of it for a radar cross section measurement "pole" fly-off. Lockheed's design advanced.

In April 1976, after winning the radar measurement pole fly-off, a joint U.S. Air Force and Defense Advanced Research Projects Agency contract was awarded to the Skunk Works to develop, build, flight-test, and evaluate two XST air vehicles by using, for the most part, off-the-shelf aircraft components including an in-production powerplant. The first XST was to demonstrate and validate the type's flying characteristics, whereas the second XST was to demonstrate and validate the type's radar and infrared signatures or, hopefully, lack thereof.

The Skunk Works' criteria for building its two Have Blue XST demonstration and validation air vehicles included the following:

- Build them small and light—about one-third the actual size of a production airplane.
- Employ a single-seat cockpit with a proven ejection seat system.
- Use as many off-the-shelf aircraft components as possible to speed development time and reduce cost.
- Employ two nonaugmented (nonafterburning) General Electric J85 turbojet engines.
- Employ no tactical equipment (identification, friend or foe [IFF] devices; inflight refueling capability; weapons bay, and so on).
- Develop and produce improved radar-absorbing material and a better way to apply it.

It was time to build the two Have Blue XST air vehicles, already designed. Lockheed's Skunk Works had developed a plane unlike any plane seen before. Instead of curves, it had angles. It featured highly sweptback wings and two inboard-canted vertical tails, and its engines were mounted atop its wings. But, if all came about as planned, its shape alone promised to reduce its radar cross section by as much as 85 percent.

Building by hand without permanent alignment jigs, Skunk Works technicians secretly assembled the two Have Blue XST air vehicles in a cordoned-off area within Lockheed's Burbank facility. The air vehicles received neither U.S. Air Force serial

numbers nor Department of Defense designations. Lockheed, however, issued its own build numbers to them: 1001 and 1002.

The Have Blue XST air vehicles were small and light. They came with a 22 foot wingspan; 38 foot length, excluding their nose boom; 7.5 foot height; and 12,000 pound gross weight. The leading edge of their semidelta wings was swept aftward 72.5 degrees (5 degrees more than that on the F-117A), and instead of outward-canted twin vertical tails (like those on the F-117A), they featured twin fins canted 30 degrees inward from the

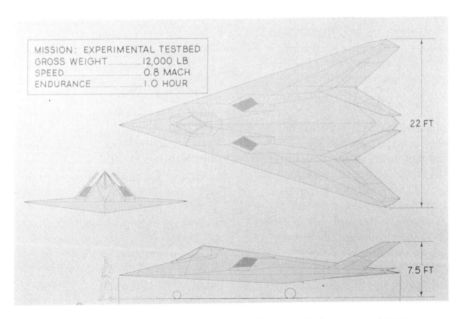

MISSION: EXPERIMENTAL TESTBED
GROSS WEIGHT_____12,000 LB
SPEED_____0.8 MACH
ENDURANCE_____1.0 HOUR

22 FT

7.5 FT

Drawing of the Have Blue XST general arrangement shows the air vehicle's jewel- and prism-cut faceted design.

The aircraft features a highly swept-back semidelta wing planform. Department of Defense

vertical, these being swept back 35 degrees at their leading edge. They incorporated Northrop F-5 landing gear, cockpit instrumentation, and ejection seats. Maximum speed was Mach 0.8, and endurance was 1 hour. Their wings featured two inboard trailing edge elevons for pitch and roll control; the all-movable rudders provided yaw control.

For comparison, the XST air vehicles were some 21 feet narrower, 5 feet lower, 28 feet shorter, and 40,500 pounds lighter than the production F-117A, but generally similar in overall appearance. Have Blue aircraft, however, employed V-type cockpit canopy windshields (a la the F-102 and F-106), whereas the F-117A uses a three-piece flat plate wind screen.

The first Have Blue XST air vehicle was completed in November 1977, two years after program go-ahead. It was subsequently loaded, with wings removed, aboard a Lockheed C-5 transport and flown to the highly classified Groom Lake flight test area in the Nellis Air Force Base test range complex. Earlier, Lockheed chose Bill Park to serve as chief test pilot on the Have Blue program, and the U.S. Air Force selected Lieutenant Colonel Norman Kenneth ("Ken") Dyson—later chief test pilot at Rockwell's North American Aircraft, flying the Rockwell–MBB X-31A enhanced fighter maneuverability

aircraft—to serve as its project pilot.

Skunk Works technicians equipped both XST air vehicles with the latest fly-by-wire flight control system from the General Dynamics F-16A Fighting Falcon, which was modified to make the Have Blue aircraft stable about all three axes (the F-16 is only unstable about the pitch axis).

After arrival, assembly, and systems checks, the first XST completed a series of low- and medium-speed taxi trials. Then, in December 1977, Park made its successful first flight. Flight testing proceeded better than expected for about four months, considering the type's inherent instability; excellent piloting and the F-16's modified fly-by-wire flight control system made the difference. As had been predicted during wind tunnel evaluations, the XST airplane had a very high landing speed—about 240 miles per hour—owing to its semidelta wing configuration and its lack of flaps and speed brakes.

Following yet another successful test hop on 4 May 1978, flight test number thirty-six, Park attempted to make a landing. But, as fate would have it, the aircraft reminded everyone about its high landing speed. One of the XST's main landing gears hit the runway too hard. The force of impact caused it to move into a half-extended–half-retracted configuration. Park made several attempts to free the jammed gear by impacting the other main landing gear onto the runway. He hoped to free up the stuck gear in this fashion so that it would either retract for a possible belly landing or extend and lock for a normal landing—but to no avail. Thus, he was authorized to climb to a safe altitude—reportedly 10,000 feet—for an emergency bailout.

After blowing the cockpit canopy, Park ejected, but he somehow hit his head and was knocked unconscious. He was still unconscious when he hit the ground, and since he was unable to control his parachute descent or landing, he sustained severe back injuries on impact—unfortunately, severe enough that he had to take an early retirement from flying. But Park stayed on at Lockheed and became director of flight operations, a position he held until his retirement in 1989.

Have Blue XST number one—the flight test and evaluation airplane—was a total loss. It was secretly disposed of somewhere in the Nellis Air Force Base test range complex. Have Blue XST number two—the low-observable technology demonstrator—arrived shortly after the demise of number one. Its first flight, with Lieutenant Colonel Ken Dyson at the controls, came about in June 1978.

Have Blue XST number one proved that a faceted air vehicle could indeed fly, as had been predicted in wind tunnel tests, but it was up to Have Blue XST number two to demonstrate and validate that the type could survive—that is, fly against various radar systems (ground-to-air, air-to-air, and air-to-ground) and present such a tiny radar cross section that it would not be detected by any radar system at tactically useful distances. In addition, it had to undergo infrared (heat) detection tests.

During fifty-one low-observable demonstration and validation test flights, flown between June 1978 and July 1979, the type proved its survivability. Then, during flight number fifty-two in July 1979, XST number two was lost.

One of the XST's hydraulic fluid line welds cracked, spraying fluid on the hot section of an engine. The fluid caught fire, and the subsequent flames grew intense. With a fire onboard that could not be extinguished, and with the loss of hydraulic power, Dyson was cleared to abandon the aircraft. He made a successful emergency ejection and a good parachute landing. But, like XST number one, XST number two was a total loss; it too was disposed of somewhere in the Nellis Air Force Base test range complex.

No additional Have Blue XSTs were needed or built, since the first of five full-scale development Senior Trend or F-117 stealth fighter aircraft would soon be under construction.

XST Specifications

Type	Single-seat, twin-engine experimental survivable testbed air vehicle
Wingspan	22 feet, 0 inches
Wing area	Unknown
Length	38 feet (without nose boom)
Height	7 feet, 5 inches
Empty weight	Unknown
Maximum weight	12,000 pounds
Maximum speed	Mach 0.8
Service ceiling	Unknown
Rate of climb	Unknown
Maximum range	Unknown (1-hour endurance)
Armament	None
Powerplant	2 nonafterburning General Electric J85 turbojet engines (specific model unknown)

Have Blue XST Production

Designation	Build Number
XST-1	1001
XST-2	1002

Chapter 17

F-117A Black Jet

We painted them [F-117s] black because the TAC [Tactical Air Command] commander wanted them black. The Skunk Works plays by the Golden Rule: he who has the gold sets the rules! If the general had wanted pink, we'd have painted them pink.

—Ben Rich

Following its submission in mid-1978 of two different low-observable, or stealth, technology aircraft based on the Have Blue testbed configuration—one a fighter resembling the F-117A, the other a midsize bomber about the same size of a B-58 Hustler—the Skunk Works was awarded an official U.S. Air Force go-ahead on Project Senior Trend. Thus, on 16 November 1978, it was awarded a contract to build five full-scale development (FSD) and fifteen production examples of the fighter. The proposed bomber had a two-person crew and four engines, but otherwise was very similar to the F-117A configuration. The FSD aircraft are essentially preproduction F-117A aircraft used for flight-test and evaluation and for low-observable and weapons delivery tests; three are still being used for ongoing tests,

one (number one, tail number 780) is pylon-mounted at Nellis Air Force Base, Nevada, and another (number two, tail number 781) has been retired to the U.S. Air Force Museum at Wright-Patterson Air Force Base; it arrived there on 17 July 1991.

F-117A Development

To develop and build the first five FSD F-117A aircraft, besides increasing size and weight values, many revisions and additions had to be engineered and put to work. These, in part, included the following:

• Reengineered cockpit and cockpit canopy
• Redesigned vertical tails
• Revised propulsion system; revised engine air inlets and engine exhaust outlets
• Incorporation of a weapons bay,

First F-117A flight-test airplane shows symmetrical pitot tubes on its nose in addition to a rounded flight-test nose boom on center line. At the time this photograph was taken, Lockheed test pilots Hal Farley, Skip Holm, and Dave Ferguson were on its pilot roster. The five flight-test F-117A aircraft, all full-scale development aircraft, were dubbed Scorpion 1 through Scorpion 5 (tail numbers 780 through 784); Scorpion 1 is shown in an overall gray paint scheme. Lockheed

weapons racks, and weapons delivery systems

• Employment of new and off-the-shelf tactical avionics

• Addition of a parachute braking system and arresting hook

• Incorporation of a wet wing within the fuel system

• Addition of an antiicing wiper blade system for the engine air inlet grids

• Employment of retractable antennas, a revolving inflight refueling receptacle, and formation and anticollision lights

• Application of improved stealth technologies as they were made

In early June 1981, the first Senior Trend FSD F-117A aircraft—minus its wings—was delivered to a secret test range within the vast boundaries of Nellis Air Force Base by means of a Lockheed C-5 Galaxy. After the aircraft was reassembled, it was prepared for its initial flight-test

Prior to the start of assembly line activities, a full-scale F-117A mockup was constructed in 1979; mockup was made from wood. The spacious forward-looking infrared bay is noteworthy. Lockheed

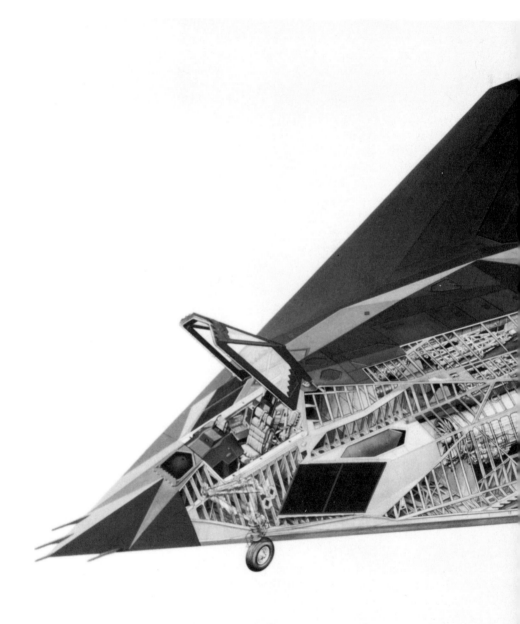

F-117A cutaway drawing shows power-plant air inlet, powerplant, and power-plant exhaust outlet configuration to good advantage. Note two precision-guided bombs in weapons bay. Lock-heed; Jim Speas

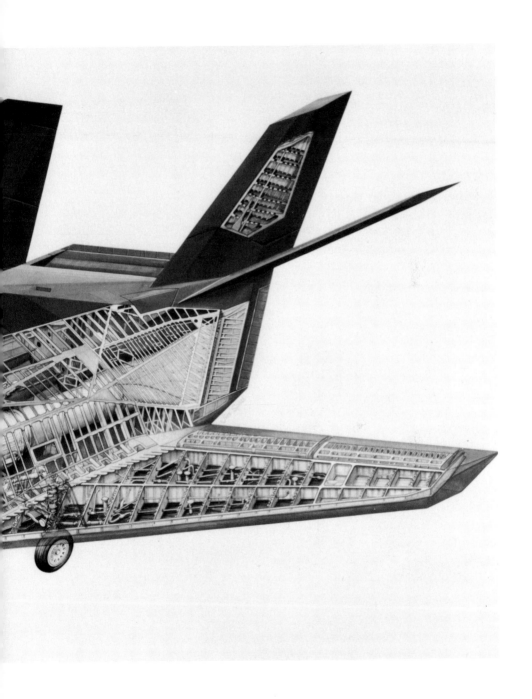

and subsequent evaluations. Lockheed selected Harold C. ("Hal") Farley to serve as chief test pilot on the F-117A stealth fighter program.

On 18 June 1981, Ship 780 rolled out of its special hanger for its first flight. Farley proceeded to make a successful first flight early that morning. During mid-1981 and early 1982, the other four FSD F-117As (Ships 781 through 784) were successfully flown. All went well until April 1982, when the

F-117A cockpit instrumentation is similar to other current fighters, with exception of the large video display monitor in the center that shows infrared images produced by the aircraft's forward-looking and downward-looking infrared units. Lockheed

first production F-117A arrived. It was ready for its first flight on 20 April.

On that day, in preparation for that first flight, Lockheed test pilot Robert L. ("Bob") Riedenauer lined up for takeoff. But unknown to him—or anyone else, apparently—some cables that operated the plane's flying control surfaces had been installed incorrectly; that is, pitch was yaw, and vice versa. Riedenauer advanced the throttles, released the brakes, and powered ahead to rotation speed and takeoff. The airplane rotated as planned, but immediately after liftoff, just after its main landing gear cleared the runway, it went berserk. Instead of its nose pitching upward, it yawed horizontally, and loss of control was instantaneous. Riedenauer had no time to correct the errant

action of the brand-new airplane or to eject from it. Mere seconds after liftoff, the airplane flew into the ground. Riedenauer was injured severely, and after his recovery, he was forced to retire from flying. The first production F-117A was damaged beyond repair, and since it had crashed prior to its delivery, it was not accepted by the U.S. Air Force; a portion of this plane's parts were used in a mockup.

The 4450th Tactical Group, which had been secretly formed on 15 October 1979 as the sole operator of the F-117A, under the command of Colonel Robert A. Jackson, achieved initial operational capability on 28 October 1983 with U.S. Air Force acceptance of production F-117A number fifteen; at this time, the group was under the guidance of its second commander, Colonel

Full-scale development F-117A number five releases a GBU-27 during separation tests. Lockheed

Harold C. ("Hal") Farley, former director of flight operations and chief test pilot for Lockheed's Skunk Works, retired in 1991. Farley joined Lockheed in 1979 as an experimental test pilot assigned to be project pilot on the top-secret stealth fighter program. He participated in all phases of the F-117A project—including design, first flight (FSD F-117A number one, U.S. Air Force serial number 79-0780), and structural, flutter, weapon separation, and weapons system testing—and has logged more than 600 hours in F-117A aircraft. He has 30 years of flying experience with a total flight time of 5,700 hours, 3,600 of which were flight tests in fighter or attack aircraft. For example, while employed by Grumman between 1967 and 1979, this former U.S. Navy experimental test pilot logged over 900 hours in the F-14 Tomcat. Farley earned his naval aviator wings in 1960. Lockheed

James S. Allen. Continued operations, all of which occurred during nighttime, with little or no moon, went relatively smooth until 11 July 1986.

On the night of 11 July, while flying production F-117A number eight, tail number 792, Major Ross E. Mulhare crashed into a small mountain some 17 miles northeast of Bakersfield, California. Major Mulhare was killed, apparently making no attempt to eject, and his airplane was destroyed by the impact. A definite cause of the crash was not publically disclosed, but disorientation was a strong possibility.

A second crash occurred on 14 October 1987. That night, while flying production F-117A number thirty-one, tail number 815, Major Michael C. Stewart crashed somewhere within the Nellis Air Force Base test range complex. He too was killed and apparently made no move to eject. Once again, the official cause was not disclosed to the public, but disorientation was likely.

Those two tragic deaths, along with the need to integrate the F-117A weapons system into its operational plans, forced the U.S. Air Force to initiate daytime as well as nighttime flying missions. To accomplish this, since the stealth fighter is not invisible to the eye, its existence had to be publically disclosed. This announcement was scheduled to occur in January 1988, but internal Pentagon pressure forced a ten-month delay.

Finally, after years of media speculation that indeed a stealth fighter did exist in squadron strength, spokesman Dan Howard of the Department of Defense held a press conference on 10 November 1988 at the Pentagon. There, with the official release of a single poor-quality photograph and very few details, the actual existence of the long-rumored stealth fighter was verified.

Surprisingly, the airplane was not at all curvaceous, as had been assumed all along. Instead, it was just the reverse: angular and jutted. All previous artist's concepts and a popular plastic model kit depicting the elusive airplane became obsolete in an instant.

The aircraft's official designation, assumed to be F-19, was in fact F-117—a complete surprise! Since no airplane with the designation F-19 existed between the McDonnell Douglas F/A-18 Hornet and the Northrop F-20 Tigershark, this assumption had been logical. The F-117 designation was a clever ploy, too, because after the General Dynamics F-111, no more Century Series designations were issued to fighter aircraft.

In retrospect, about the only thing that was *not* a huge surprise was that the stealth fighter was indeed a product of the Skunk Works. The U.S. Air Force, whose number one priority had been

An F-117A takeoff sequence. This
F-117A left Nellis Air Force Base's main
complex to return to Tonopah Test
Range after coming back to the United
States from Saudi Arabia following
Operation Desert Storm. Tony Landis

Rare side-by-side view of the Skunk Works' two newest creations: the

F-117A stealth fighter and the F-22 advanced tactical fighter. Lockheed

program security since day one, has to be congratulated for keeping a lid on its stealth fighter program for more than ten years.

The 4450th Tactical Group was disestablished on 5 October 1989, and at the same time, its successor, the 37th Tactical Fighter Wing (later 49th Fighter Wing), was established. The 4450th, when terminated, had four squadrons: I-Unit, 4450th Test Squadron (TS), the Nightstalkers; P-Unit, 4451st TS; Q-Unit, 4452nd TS, the Goatsuckers; and Z-Unit, 4453rd Test and Evaluation Squadron, the Grim Reapers. Units I and Q operated production F-117As, Z-Unit operated the five FSD F-117As, and P-Unit operated a number of Ling-Temco-Vought (LTV) A-7D Corsair IIs for chase and training duties. This mix of aircraft was maintained for a time after the formation of the 37th, but Northrop T-38A and AT-38B

Talons later replaced the A-7s. Moreover, units I, Z, and Q were soon redesignated the 415th, 416th, and 417th Fighter Squadrons respectively. P-Unit was disbanded when the 37th Tactical Fighter Wing was established.

The 415th kept I-Unit's nickname, the Nightstalkers. The 416th did not retain its predecessor's nickname; it became the Ghostriders. The 417th dropped its predecessor's nickname, becoming the Bandits. At the time, the 37th Fighter Wing was under the command of Colonel (now Brigadier General) Anthony J. ("Tony") Tolin, the group's and wing's sixth commander.

A giant aerospace media event occurred on 21 April 1990 at both Nellis Air Force Base's main complex and the Pentagon, when the Department of Defense released more details on the

Spectacular overhead view of an F-117A and its surroundings at Tonopah Test Range, circa 1990.

Lockheed; Eric Schulzinger; Denny Lombard

F-117A, ten high-quality photographs, and an 8-minute video. Simultaneously, at Nellis Air Force Base, two F-117As were put on public display for the first time. At this point, the 37th had fifty-six operational F-117As on hand. On 12 July 1990, in a ceremony at Lockheed's Plant 10 facility at U.S. Air Force Plant 42, the fifty-ninth and last production F-117A was delivered to the U.S. Air Force at Palmdale.

Flying the F-117A, according to pilot reports, is a pleasure. The aircraft is easy to fly and not a "wobblin' goblin" by current measures, although early on, before its fly-by-wire flight control system was perfected, its nose had a tendency to "hunt" (i.e., oscillate). It is said to handle very much like the McDonnell Douglas F-15 Eagle, which, like the F-117A, has light wing loading and is very maneuverable. The F-117A,

The seventh production F-117A, tail number 793, prepares to taxi outside its special hangar at Tonopah Test *Range, circa 1990. Lockheed; Eric Schulzinger; Denny Lombard*

however, owing to its design, has a normal sink rate but high landing speed that compares to that of the General Dynamics (Convair) F-106 Delta Dart: some 240 miles per hour plus. For this reason, in part, the stealth fighter has a large braking drag parachute: about 18 feet in diameter. Its parabrake is deployed as soon as the nose landing gear wheel makes contact with a runway. This action helps to

The F-117A Colonel Anthony J. ("Tony") Tolin, former commander of the 37th Tactical Fighter Wing, is prepared for flight inside its Tonopah Test Range hangar, circa 1990. Lockheed; Eric Schulzinger; Denny Lombard

Current F-117As are not capable of all-weather operations. Instead, they are optimized for in-weather operations—that is, flying through clouds to help them elude detection. Lockheed; Eric Schulzinger; Denny Lombard

241

Beautiful inflight view of an F-117A over snow-capped mountains. Lock- *heed; Eric Schulzinger; Denny Lombard*

slow down the fast-rolling aircraft and to help reduce excessive wear on the wheel brakes and tires. The drag chute doubles as an antispin device if the aircraft should ever enter a spin.

Another flying pleasure for F-117A pilots is the aircraft's hallmark GE F404 turbofan engine. It is responsive, reliable, and it has adequate thrust for the stealth fighter's high-subsonic-speed regime (Mach 0.8).

The F-117A's flying surfaces include four elevons (combined elevators and ailerons; two inboard and two outboard) on the trailing edge of either wing, and two all-movable rudders (one atop either fixed vertical tail stub). The four elevons deflect upward and downward about 60 degrees, and the two rudders deflect left and right some 30 degrees. The elevons

are split into four segments because of their large area and do not act as flaps; they operate in concert as two elevons (one on the trailing edge of either wing) during flight. The all-movable rudders are one-piece, and each pivots on a single post protruding from either fixed vertical tail stub. The elevons provide control about the pitch and roll axes, and the rudders provide control about the yaw axis. To help reduce the aircraft's high landing speed, the angle of attack for its runway approach and landing touchdown is 9.5 degrees. The aircraft's flat bottom is not based on the lifting body theory, as has been reported in other references, but is for stealth characteristics alone.

The mission of the stealth fighter is to strike and destroy high-value targets, in a precise manner, with any conventional or

Close-up view of an F-117A being re-
fueled inflight by a KC-10 Extender.
Mike Machat Illustration

Left-side profile of an F-117A with a 49th Fighter Wing (formerly 37th   Fighter Wing) T-38 Talon. Mike Machat Illustration

nuclear device that will fit within the F-117A's internal weapons bay. Strategic targets such as radar installations, command and control bunkers, hardened aircraft hangars, and surface-to-surface and surface-to-air guided missile sites are among the Black Jet's primary prey. It can carry and deliver precision-guided ordnance. Located within its V-shaped belly, on its centerline, the F-117A's internal weapons bay features two inboard-opening doors. The weapons bay is long, wide, and deep enough to provide adequate volume for a variety of tactical ordnance—some unclassified. These include two laser-guided Mk84 2,000 pound bombs; two laser-guided GBU-10 Paveway II 2,000 pound bombs; two laser-guided GBU-12 Paveway II 500 pound bombs; two laser-guided GBU-27 Paveway III 2,000 pound bombs, which are BLU-109B *improved* 2,000 pound Mk84s

with the Paveway III guidance system; and unspecified nuclear devices.

The stealth fighter (nicknamed "Ghost" in the Gulf War) is not optimized for contemporary self-defense. That is, it has neither onboard cannons nor air-to-air guided missiles for its own protection. Instead, it simply relies on its stealth technology for its survival when in action. This was proven on a day-to-day basis during Operation Desert Storm, and its continual tactical surprise during that operation was due for the most part to the extreme difficulties any air defense has in detecting it. Furthermore, as now proven, its laser-guided bombs strike targets with precise accuracy.

The F-117A is not only a deadly warplane, it is an award winner. In 1989, Ben Rich, retired Chief Skunk and consultant to the Skunk Works, as well as the entire

Lockheed and U.S. Air Force F-117A weapons system team received the Robert J. Collier Trophy for 1988. This trophy, which is presented annually by the National Aeronautic Association, is the most prestigious in American aviation. It indicates the "greatest achievement in aeronautics or astronautics in America, with respect to improving the performance, efficiency, and safety of air or space vehicles, the value of which has been thoroughly demonstrated by actual use during the preceding year."

Earlier, in 1988, the 4450th Tactical Group was awarded the Tactical Air Command (now part of the Air Combat Command) Commander's Maintenance Award in the Special Mission category.

In September 1989, three of the F-117A's main creators—Alan Brown (former Lockheed Corporation director of engineering; now retired), C. R. "Dick" Cantrell (former senior technical advisor on the F-22 advanced tactical fighter program, now retired), and Norm Nelson (retired Skunk Works vice-president and general manager)—received the design award of the American Institute of Aeronautics and Astronautics.

Finally, the 37th Fighter Wing has earned superior ratings during U.S. Air Force operational readiness inspections.

These awards are sure to be followed by others. And these awards give credit to the clever engineers and hard workers within the Skunk Works that labored as a team to create the unique Lockheed F-117A Black Jet (the unofficial nickname its pilots prefer), the world's first stealth fighter.

In early May 1992, an F-117A that had been modified with a number of system upgrades, was displayed during U.S. Air Force Plant 42's Salute to Youth Day. Its modifications included the installation of new avionics and improvements to the F404 engine exhaust system, which, according to Program Manager Paul Martin, "has become one of the most burdensome areas on the plane." The plane also features composite weapons bay doors. Before deployment for Operation Desert Shield, a retrofit program was begun to install composite rudders on the entire fleet of F-117As. This program began after one of the metal rudders began fluttering and fell off an F-117A. This program is now completed. Jack Gordon, vice-president of the Skunk Works, reported that the rudder retrofit had been performed on about half the F-117A fleet when deployment to Saudi Arabia for the Gulf War interrupted the program. Finally, with its new avionics, the stealth fighter's offensive capability has been largely enhanced.

On 1 June 1992, Holloman Air Force Base, New Mexico, became

the new home of the F-117A. Simultaneously, the 37th Fighter Wing was disestablished. Since the fleet of F-117As has replaced the 49th Fighter Wing's fleet of F-15 Eagles at Holloman, the fleet of F-117s now fly under the standard of the 49th Fighter Wing. It remains unclear, however, under what fighter squadron's banners the F-117s will operate. The 49th Fighter Wing's three fighter squadrons, which were still listed as the 7th, 8th, and 9th, may transform into the 415th, 416th, and 417th Fighter Squadrons.

Key Contributors

Lockheed's Skunk Works produced four key contributors to the design and development of the F-117A stealth fighter. These are Alan Brown, Dick Cantrell, Jack Gordon, and Norm Nelson.

Alan Brown, now retired, began his aeronautical career with an engineering apprenticeship at Blackburn Aircraft in England from 1945 to 1950. He joined Lockheed in 1960, starting in the physics laboratory of the research and development division of Lockheed Missiles and Space

An F-117A arrives at Langley Air Force Base, Virginia, before departure to Saudi Arabia in support of Operation Desert Shield; the large braking parachute is some 18 feet in diameter. In the background are 16 earlier arrivals. In all, 43 F-117As participated in Operation Desert Storm with an 85 percent mission capable rate. U.S. Air Force

Norman E. ("Norm") Nelson received the American Institute of Aeronautics and Astronautics Aircraft Design Award for his contribution to the design of the F-117. Lockheed

Jack S. Gordon was appointed executive vice-president of the Skunk Works on 8 May 1990. Lockheed

Company. He moved to Burbank in 1966, working on propulsion installation on Lockheed's SST and the FX and VSX aircraft (which became the F-15 Eagle and S-3 Viking respectively), and was engineering manager for Lockheed at Rolls-Royce in England on the Lockheed L-1011 wide-body commercial transport program.

Among Brown's responsibilities before his retirement in 1991 was the development of concurrent engineering within Lockheed Corporation. Previously, he was for several years director of low-observable technology at Lockheed Aeronautical Systems Company in Burbank (now in Marietta). From 1978 to 1982, he was the program manager and the chief engineer on the F-117A program, and since 1975, he had been active in stealth technology programs.

Brown has master's degrees in aeronautical engineering from

The General Electric F404-GE-F1D2 nonafterburning engine is employed by all F-117A aircraft. For the most part, *the marriage of this engine to the stealth fighter has been trouble free.* General Electric

Full-scale development F-117A number four—Scorpion 4 (tail number 783)— *at an Edwards AFB open house static display, circa 1991. Tony Landis*

Cranfield Institute of Technology, England, and Stanford University, California, and is a fellow of the Royal Aeronautical Society and an associate fellow of the American Institute of Aeronautics and Astronautics. He received the American Institute of Aeronautics and Astronautics Aircraft Design Award for 1990 for his contribution to the design of the F-117.

Dick Cantrell joined Lockheed in 1954 as an aerodynamics engineer. For much of his career, he worked in the Skunk Works, where he was appointed director of flight sciences in 1980 and director of engineering and programs in 1984. In January 1989, Cantrell was named senior technical advisor on Lockheed's advanced tactical fighter program; he had been director of engineering on that program since July 1987. He received the

American Institute of Aeronautics and Astronautics Aircraft Design Award for 1990 for his contribution to the design of the F-117.

Jack Gordon, executive vice-president of the Skunk Works, joined Advanced Development Projects in 1964 as a propulsion engineer. During his career, he participated in the design of the SR-71, U-2R (formerly TR-1), and the F-117. He has held a number of executive positions in the Skunk Works, including deputy program manager on a classified program, F-117 chief engineer, and program director for Lockheed's F-22. Gordon was named executive vice-president of Lockheed Advanced Development Company on 8 May 1990 when the company was created out of the Advanced Development Projects division of Lockheed Aeronautical Systems Company; he had been Advanced

Dramatic view of an F-117A lifting-off from Nellis' main base area on its return flight to Tonopah Test Range after its return from Saudi Arabia. Tony Landis

Development Projects' assistant general manager since December 1987 and was named a Lockheed Aeronautical Systems Company vice-president in March 1989.

Norm Nelson, who retired in January 1987 as vice-president and general manager of the Skunk Works, had rejoined Lockheed as a Skunk Works project director in January 1976. In 1979, he became the Skunk Works' vice-president for engineering and program management, directing all engineering, research, and development. In 1984, Nelson was appointed the Skunk Works' vice-president and general manager. He received the American Institute of Aeronautics and Astronautics Aircraft Design Award for 1990 for his contribution to the design of the F-117.

F-117A Specifications

Type	Single-seat, twin-engine strike fighter
Wingspan	43 feet, 4 inches
Wing area	Classified
Length	65 feet, 11 inches
Height	12 feet, 5 inches
Empty weight	28,500 pounds
Maximum weight	52,500 pounds
Maximum speed	Mach 0.8
Service ceiling	Classified
Rate of climb	Classified
Maximum range	900 miles (without inflight refueling)
Armament	Conventional laser-guided bombs; tactical munitions dispensers; nuclear bombs
Powerplant	2 General Electric nonafterburning 10,000 pound-thrust class F404-GE-F1D2 turbofan engines

F-117A Production

Designation	Serial Number	Comments
F-117A (FSD-1)	79-01780	First flown 18 June 1981; now mounted on pylon near U.S. Air Force Red Flag Headquarters at Nellis Air Force Base, Nevada
F-117A (FSD-2)	79-01781	On display at U.S. Air Force Museum at Wright-Patterson Air Force Base, Dayton, Ohio; arrived 17 July 1991
F-117A (FSD-3)	79-01782	Used for ongoing developments
F-117A (FSD-4)	79-01783	Used for ongoing developments
F-117A (FSD-5)	79-01784	Used for ongoing developments
F-117A	none	Crashed 20 April 1982 prior to U.S. Air Force acceptance; not counted in F-117A production total
F-117A-1	80-01785	First production F-117A
F-117A-2	80-01786	
F-117A-3	80-01787	
F-117A-4	80-01788	
F-117A-5	80-01789	
F-117A-6	80-01790	
F-117A-7	80-01791	
F-117A-8	81-01792	Crashed 11 July 1986; Ross Mulhare killed; aircraft a total loss
F-117A-9	81-01793	
F-117A-10	81-01794	
F-117A-11	81-01795	
F-117A-12	81-01796	
F-117A-13	81-01797	
F-117A-14	81-01798	
F-117A-15	82-01799	With delivery of this F-117A on 28 October 1983, the 4450th Tactical Group achieved initial operational capability
F-117A-16	82-01800	
F-117A-17	82-01801	
F-117A-18	82-01802	
F-117A-19	82-01803	
F-117A-20	82-01804	
F-117A-21	82-01805	
F-117A-22	82-01806	
F-117A-23	82-01807	
F-117A-24	83-01808	Only F-117A with fiscal year 1983 prefix
F-117A-25	84-01809	
F-117A-26	84-01810	

Designation	Serial Number	Comments
F-117A-27	84-01811	
F-117A-28	84-01812	
F-117A-29	85-01813	Flown by 49th Fighter Wing commander
F-117A-30	85-01814	
F-117A-31	85-01815	Crashed 14 October 1987; Michael Stewart killed; aircraft a total loss
F-117A-32	85-01816	
F-117A-33	85-01817	
F-117A-34	85-01818	
F-117A-35	85-01819	
F-117A-36	85-01820	
F-117A-37	85-01821	
F-117A-38	85-01822	
F-117A-39	85-01823	
F-117A-40	84-01824	
F-117A-41	84-01825	
F-117A-42	84-01826	
F-117A-43	84-01827	
F-117A-44	84-01828	
F-117A-45	85-01829	
F-117A-46	85-01830	
F-117A-47	85-01831	
F-117A-48	85-01832	
F-117A-49	85-01833	
F-117A-50	85-01834	
F-117A-51	85-01835	
F-117A-52	85-01836	
F-117A-53	86-01837	
F-117A-54	86-01838	3 complete 18-plane F-117A fighter squadrons, 1 F-117A fighter wing, established with delivery of this airplane
F-117A-55	86-01839	
F-117A-56	86-01840	
F-117A-57	87-01841	
F-117A-58	87-01842	
F-117A-59	87-01843	59th and last production F-117A; delivered 12 July 1990

Note: five full-scale development F-117As were financed in fiscal year 1979; seven production F-117As were financed in fiscal year 1980; seven in fiscal year 1981; nine in fiscal year 1982; one in fiscal year 1983; nine in fiscal year 1984; nineteen in fiscal year 1985; four in fiscal year 1986, and three in fiscal year 1987.

F-22 Lightning II

Looking back at five Lockheed Skunk Works programs—the YF-12, the SR-71, Have Blue, the F-117 and the F-22—the average time from go-ahead to first flight was twenty-seven months.

—Lawrence M. Harris, Kemper Securities

Unofficially named Lightning II, the F-22 advanced tactical fighter is scheduled to begin replacing the McDonnell Douglas F-15 Eagle in the year 2002 when the F-22 is projected to meet its initial operational capability with the U.S. Air Force Air Combat Command; the U.S. Air Force plans to procure 648 F-22 aircraft.

The F-15 achieved its initial operational capability in 1975 with the First Fighter Wing at Langley Air Force Base, Virginia. Since 1975, many U.S. Air Force fighter wings, and their respective fighter squadrons, have continued to receive and operate the highly respected and very efficient Eagle. Without a doubt, it remains a premier air superiority fighter type. Its extraordinary tenure with the U.S. Air Force cannot last forever, however. First flown in 1972, the Eagle continues to demonstrate its prowess as a fully

missionized tactical fighter. Its contemporaries worldwide, however, are beginning to match its capabilities. By the early 2000s, it will no longer be matchless. Hence the U.S. Air Force's need for the F-22 weapons system, which it believes will be a 100 percent improvement over the F-15 weapons system.

F-22 Development

It was late 1983 when the U.S. Air Force began looking for the F-15's future replacement. The U.S. Air Force then solicited design concepts from the industry for what it called the advanced tactical fighter. By mid-1984, seven airframe contractors—Boeing, General Dynamics, Grumman, Lockheed, McDonnell Douglas, Northrop, and Rockwell—had all submitted their respective design concepts to the Advanced Tactical Fighter Weapon System Program

Office at Wright-Patterson Air Force Base. Then, each firm received a contract valued at about $1 million to further its studies.

Simultaneously, a pair of powerplant contractors—General Electric and Pratt & Whitney—were selected to participate in the advanced tactical fighter program under a fifty-month-long joint advanced fighter engine program,

each firm being awarded an identical $202 million contract.

Prospective advanced tactical fighter airframe contractors had to integrate the best overall features of current, and forthcoming, technologies into their designs. The winning design would be the one that achieved the best integration of these known and classified technologies into a well-

Arthur M. James, program manager for contract research and development at Lockheed's Composite Development Center, inspects spools of dry fiber material on their way to a resin bath (left center) and prior to being pulled through heated die. The die will con- *solidate and shape the material into a solid part for an aircraft. This manu-facturing technique, known as "pultru-sion," is one of several methods being studied at Lockheed for the construc-tion of aircraft with composite mate-rials. Lockheed*

balanced air superiority fighter weapon system. Possible applications included very high-speed integrated circuit technology; common avionics modules; high-speed data buses; shared low-observable antennas; a 1750 computer with Ada software; integrated electronic warfare system technology; advanced data fusion cockpit display screens; integrated communications, navigation, and identification avionics technology; fiber-optics data transmission; active wing camber control; high-pressure and nonflammable hydraulic fluid systems; hydraulically actuated weapons racks; voice command and control; integrated flight and propulsion controls; short takeoff and landing capability; two-dimensional, thrust-vectoring, and thrust-reversing exhaust nozzles; composite materials for airframe structures, internal and external; supersonic cruise (supercruise) without engine afterburning; and low-observable, or stealth, technology characteristics. All this, and more, was to be integrated in a fighter with a gross weight of

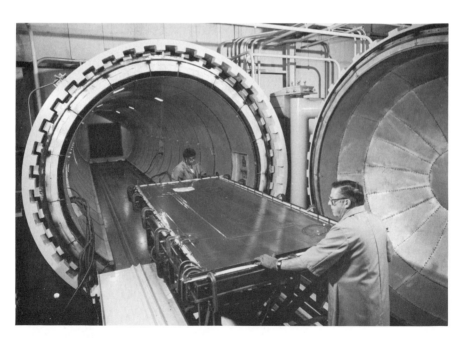

This giant autoclave at Lockheed cured advanced composite materials used on the YF-22 prototypes. Thermoplastic-resin composites are both stronger and lighter than the metal alloys used on today's fighter aircraft, and they are easily repairable. Lockheed

about 50,000 pounds and the same approximate dimensions as those of the F-15. (By 1992, the gross weight of the F-22 had risen to about 60,000 pounds—but, according to the U.S. Air Force, no gross weight limit was ever imposed on the aircraft. The aircraft remained, however, nearly equal in dimensional size to the F-15.)

All seven airframe contractors submitted their advanced tactical fighter design concepts to the system program office by 31 July 1984, as had been directed, and U.S. Air Force evaluations began in August. Three months later, the Milestone One System Acquisition Review Council program review was held, the first major program evaluation and decision point of the Department of Defense on the advanced tactical fighter program.

On 8 October 1985, the U.S. Air Force issued a formal request for proposals to the seven airframe contractors, soliciting contractor

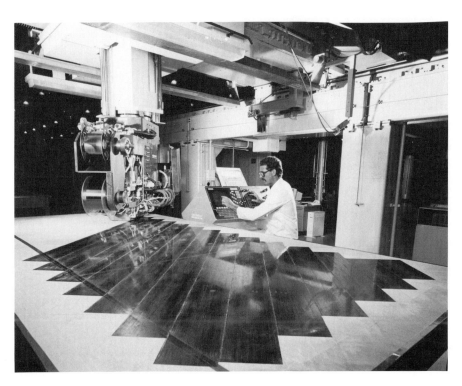

A Lockheed technician cuts strips of thermoplastic-resin composites for an aircraft panel. Lockheed

plans for the demonstration and validation phase of the advanced tactical fighter program. Technical data were due at the system program office in sixty days, and cost and price proposals were due in seventy-five days. The officials at the system program office received those data at those times, evaluated them during a six-month-long source selection, and narrowed down the number of concepts. The demonstration and validation phase included wind tunnel tests, mockup evaluations, subsystem evaluations, and man-in-the-loop simulations and supportability demonstrations leading to detailed designs suitable for full-scale development (now engineering and manufacturing development).

According to this schedule, another source selection would

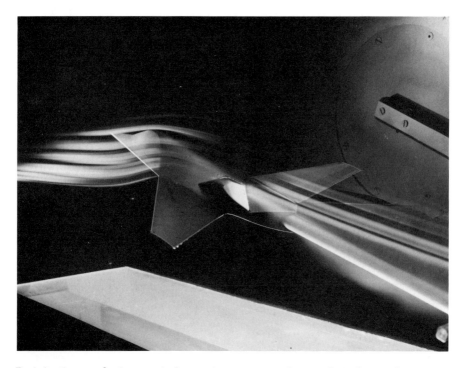

By injecting smoke into a wind tunnel and illuminating it with a laser, Lockheed engineers can see air flow patterns as they move around a model of a future fighter design such as the F-22. The Skunk Works completed more than 24,000 *hours of wind-tunnel testing to ensure that the YF-22 design met the Air Force's defined performance goals; wind-tunnel evaluations on the F-22 continue. Lockheed*

follow the demonstration and validation phase and result in the choice of a single airframe contractor or contractor team to develop, flight-test, and produce the advanced tactical fighter. That choice would be made in late 1986, with the first flight of the advanced tactical fighter occurring in 1990.

In today's high-risk aerospace business, where ongoing budget cuts continue to reduce the size of aircraft production orders, where aircraft development costs border the astronomical—witness the Northrop B-2 advanced technology bomber—it is prudent for airframe contractors to join

David L. ("Dave") Ferguson, former chief test pilot for the Lockheed YF-22 program, is now director of flight operations within the Skunk Works. Ferguson succeeded Hal Farley—the first person to fly the F-117A stealth fighter—on 1 July 1991; Ferguson was the second pilot to fly the F-117A. A decorated veteran of the Vietnam War, *where he served two tours of duty as a U.S. Air Force F-105 fighter pilot, Ferguson joined Lockheed in 1979. Previously, he flew many of the nation's most advanced fighter aircraft as a U.S. Air Force test pilot at the U.S. Air Force Flight Test Center at Edwards Air Force Base, California. Lockheed*

The first flight of the winning Pratt & Whitney YF119–powered YF-22 with

Tom Morgenfeld under glass and with landing gear extended. Lockheed

forces to share expenses, production, and profits. Of the seven competing airframe contractors, Grumman and Rockwell chose to go it alone, with the other five joining forces to make the teams of Lockheed–Boeing–General Dynamics and Northrop–McDonnell Douglas. These teaming agreements included follow-up design, manufacture, test, and support of the advanced tactical fighter, with the understanding that the winning airframe contractor would be the prime contractor, and the teammate or teammates would be the principle contractor or contractors.

On 31 October 1986, the advanced tactical fighter designs from Lockheed and Northrop were selected. They would be prime contractors, and their team members would be principle contractors. Each contractor team would build two flyable service test aircraft along with an associated testbed air vehicle. Each contractor team would also fly its advanced tactical fighters with both the General Electric and Pratt & Whitney advanced tactical fighter service test powerplants. This action began a fifty-month demonstration and validation phase to end no later than 31 December 1990, which was later upped to fifty-four months, to end no later than 30 April 1991.

At this time, the Lockheed–Boeing–General Dynamics design was designated YF-22A, and the Northrop–McDonnell Douglas design was designated YF-23A. Simultaneously, the General Electric GE37 engine was designated YF120-GE-100, and the Pratt & Whitney PW5000 engine was designated YF119-PW-100.

Lockheed and Northrop each received a fixed-price contract of

$818 million for the final demonstration and validation phase, which included flight testing and evaluation. When this phase was over, one contractor team would advance to the engineering and manufacturing development phase of the advanced tactical fighter program. Originally, this next phase, called Milestone Two, was to last about

five years and lead to the aircraft's initial operational capability in the late 1990s. But, because of the aforementioned ongoing budget cuts since then, the F-22's initial operational capability was rescheduled for 2002. The U.S. Air Force Air Combat Command had hoped to procure 750 F-22s to supplement, and ultimately replace, its F-15s, which by the

An exceptional inflight, head-on view of the YF-22 illustrates its sporty configuration. The way the leading edges *of its stabilators fit into the trailing edge wing flaps is unique. Lockheed*

time the F-22 begins to enter service, will be over twenty-five years old. Yet, already by 1992, the original number of F-22s had been reduced to 648. Who knows how many, if any, will actually be produced.

The first YF-22A was publicly unveiled on 29 August 1990 at Lockheed's Plant 10 facility at U.S. Air Force Plant 42, Palmdale; the first example was fitted with two General Electric YF120-GE-100 engines. The number one YF-22A had been scheduled for an earlier appearance, but late arrival of its engines—the YF120s—delayed the event.

As a preamble to its first flight, the number one YF-22A completed a low-speed taxi test of about 90 miles per hour on 19 September 1990; a medium-speed taxi test of about 120 miles per hour was completed on 27 September. No high-speed taxi test was conducted, since that would come about during its first takeoff in two days.

On 29 September 1990, David L. ("Dave") Ferguson, Lockheed's chief YF-22A test pilot (now chief of flight test operations), successfully flew the airplane from Palmdale Airport to Edwards Air Force Base in an 18-minute test hop. During the short flight, Ferguson attained a speed of 288 miles per hour and an altitude of 12,500 feet. After the flight, Ferguson is quoted in the November 1990 *Lockheed*

The number one, background, and number two YF-22s flying in formation, circa late 1990, show their identical external appearance; note the spin re-cover parachute apparatus on the number one YF-22. Lockheed

As shown, the number two YF-22 conducted the first missile launch during flight testing on 28 November 1990. Here, it is launching an unarmed AIM-9 Sidewinder at China Lake Naval Weapons Center in California. Lockheed

The number two YF-22 conducted the second missile launch on 20 December 1990. It is shown firing an unarmed AIM-120 at the Pacific Missile Test Center near Point Mugu, California.

This YF-22 was the only advanced tactical fighter air vehicle to demonstrate missile launches; neither Northrop–McDonnell Douglas YF-23 aircraft launched any missiles. Lockheed

Advanced Development Company Information Sheet as saying, "It was a very easy airplane to fly," adding, "I would be happy to put fuel in it and fly it this afternoon."

The number two YF-22A, powered by a pair of Pratt & Whitney YF119-PW-100 engines, made its first flight on 30 October 1990. It also was flown from Palmdale Airport—where both examples had been built—to Edwards Air Force Base, a 14-minute test hop, by Test Pilot Tom Morgenfeld of Lockheed. The short flight culminated after the airplane had reached a speed of 360 miles per hour and an altitude of 10,000 feet.

The two YF-22A aircraft went on to complete a rigorous flight test and evaluation program that ended on 31 December 1990. They flew seventy-four sorties during ninety-one days.

As a weapons system, the F-22 is designed to carry, in its three internal weapons bays, existing and planned air-to-air guided missiles—both radar guided and heat seeking. These include a full complement of short- and medium-range air-to-air guided missiles such as the AIM-9 Sidewinder, the AIM-120 advanced medium-range air-to-air missile, and the proposed advanced short-range air-to-air missile. It will also incorporate an advanced version of the rotary-action, six-barrel General Electric M61 Vulcan 20 millimeter cannon

to engage hostile targets head-on with rapidly updated gun sight data. The F-22 will carry at least eight air-to-air missiles: four short range and four medium range.

The General Electric YF120–powered number two YF-22A demonstrated successful missile launches on 4 and 20 December 1990. It successfully fired an AIM-9M Sidewinder and an AIM-120 on those dates, respectively. The AIM-9M launch was conducted by Test Pilot Jon Beesley of General Dynamics, and the AIM-120 launch was conducted by Test Pilot Tom Morgenfeld of Lockheed. Interestingly, the YF-22A's competition, the Northrop–McDonnell Douglas YF-23A Grey Ghost, did not demonstrate any missile launch exercise during its 104-day, fifty-sortie flight test program. Apparently, Lockheed and its teammates were better prepared for such activities during the YF-22A's flight test program. But in all fairness, live missile firing demonstrations were not required.

The YF-22A's configuration features a single-seat cockpit and twin (side-by-side) powerplant arrangement. It has three internal weapons bays: one on either side of the fuselage and the third in a ventral bay on the centerline. It has twin fixed, outward-canted vertical stabilizers with large-area rudders, twin all-moving horizontal tail planes that double as stabilators, and a high-visibility cockpit canopy for 360-degree viewing for the pilot. Its all-moving stabilators mount inline with the semi-trapezoid-shaped wings, actually overlapping them, and are able to interact by way of the wing's notched inboard trailing edge flaps for stabilator and wing flap clearance; in essence, they are close-coupled stabilators. The wing is swept back 48 degrees at the leading edge and swept forward about 15 degrees at the trailing edge. The wings incorporate leading edge flaps, inboard trailing edge flaps, and outboard ailerons for lift and maneuverability. The aircraft also features two-dimensional, thrust-vectoring engine exhaust nozzles for short takeoffs and landings and for improved agility and maneuverability—especially during high-angle-of-attack maneuvers.

In a period of seven flying days from 10 through 17 December 1990, the number one YF-22A performed a series of ten high-angle-of-attack flight tests that demonstrated the plane's

Test pilot Tom Morgenfeld of Lockheed tried his best to save the number two YF-22 during its wheels-up crash landing on 25 April 1992; Morgenfeld, who was able to emerge from the aircraft without help, received minor injuries. Lockheed

The number one YF-22 goes straight up to demonstrate the power of its two General Electric YF120 engines. It has been grounded, and no determination has been made as to its disposition. Note its giant engine air inlets. Lockheed

maneuverability at slow speeds and high pitch rates.

"I don't believe any other aircraft in the world could have done what we did with the YF-22," said Test Pilot Jon Beesley of General Dynamics in the November 1990 *Lockheed Advanced Development Company Information Sheet.* "We accomplished in one week what other programs set out to do in a year or more."

In those ten test flight demonstrations, flown by Beesley and Major Mark Shackelford of the U.S. Air Force, "we achieved our test objective—an unprecedented 60-degree angle of attack [nose-up]—and still had control power," Beesley said.

After an initial flight test to check out newly installed test equipment—including an antispin parachute housed in a canister—the two pilots logged 14.9 hours on nine missions. Maneuvers used to demonstrate the YF-22A's handling performance and recovery capabilities included maximum-stick 360 degree rolls, 45-degree bank-to-bank rolls, and pushovers (from nose-up to nose-down attitudes); most of the testing was done at altitudes around 35,000

The number one YF-22, equipped with a special spin recover parachute canister, demonstrated its fantastic maneuverability during a series of flight tests in December 1990. Even with this drag-producing apparatus attached, it showed that it can outmaneuver anything else in the skies. Lockheed

Operating at speeds as slow as 120 miles per hour and at angles of attack as high as 60 degrees, the number one YF-22 demonstrated that it has no maneuverability restrictions and no an-gle-of-attack limitations, according to Lockheed and U.S. Air Force test pilots that called the aircraft's performance unprecedented. Lockheed

YF-22 number two—winner of the ad-vanced tactical fighter competition. Lockheed

feet, and for test purposes, flying was done in military power (with no afterburner). According to Beesley, "Aircraft performance was stunning." He added, "Our demonstrations proved that the YF-22 has no maneuverability restrictions. . . . no angle-of-attack limit."

The Lockheed–Boeing–General Dynamics team completed test flight activities on 28 December 1990 and submitted its formal proposal to the U.S. Air Force on 31 December. The goal of the F-22 is user friendliness because the detection of enemy threats while remaining undetected by the enemy are life and death matters for a fighter pilot. But the immediate goal was to win the advanced tactical fighter competition.

Lockheed, teamed with Boeing and General Dynamics, did

just that and was selected by the U.S. Air Force on 23 April 1991 to develop its F-22 to replace the F-15 as the air superiority fighter of the future.

On 2 August 1991, the U.S. Air Force awarded a $9.55 billion engineering and manufacturing development (formerly full-scale development) contract to the F-22 team. The first flight of an engineering and manufacturing development aircraft was scheduled for mid-1995.

Simultaneously, Pratt & Whitney was given a $1.3 billion contract to develop the powerplant slated for use in the F-22, the F119.

Most of the work in the demonstration and validation phase of the F-22 program was performed at Lockheed Aeronautical Systems Company's facility in Burbank, at Boeing in Seattle, and at the Fort Worth

Division of General Dynamics, in Texas. Lockheed Aeronautical Systems Company has been relocated to Marietta, and F-22 program management and aircraft assembly operations have also been transferred to the Marietta facilities for the engineering and manufacturing development and production phases.

Lockheed's responsibilities include overseeing weapons system integration; developing and constructing all forward fuselage structures and components, including the cockpit, and the vertical tails and stabilators; and spearheading avionics architecture and functional design as well as the production of displays, controls, the air data system, and apertures.

Boeing is responsible for the development and construction of the wings and aft fuselage; installation of the engines, nozzles, and auxiliary power unit; operation of the Avionics System Integration Laboratory and the Boeing 757 Avionics Flying Laboratory; and development and integration of the training systems.

General Dynamics is responsible for developing and building all midfuselage structures, landing gear, and key systems and armament and for providing the tailored electronic warfare system; tailored communications, navigation, and identification system; stores

management systems; and inertial navigation systems.

Unexpected Crash

At about 4:20 P.M. on 25 April 1992, as Tom Morgenfeld was completing a practice approach over a runway at Edwards Air Force Base, the Pratt & Whitney YF120–powered YF-22 crashed. The airplane was on a scheduled flight test in support of the F-22 engineering and manufacturing development program.

Test pilot Morgenfeld of Lockheed had accomplished one low-altitude approach and had nearly completed a second. As he began a go-around following the second approach, the aircraft experienced severe pitch oscillations, impacted the runway with its landing gear retracted, skidded several thousand feet, and caught fire. The pilot egressed the airplane on the ground with only minor injuries.

Just before the severe oscillations, the pilot had engaged the afterburners and retracted the landing gear.

The U.S. Air Force had no plans in 1992 to conduct additional flight testing until the first flight of the first production F-22 in 1995. The YF-22 that crashed had completed more than 90 percent of the flight test objectives while flying about 75 percent of the flight hours and sorties that were budgeted; its testing was to conclude in May 1992.

The F-22 of 2002

In late 1991, the final external design configuration of the Lockheed–Boeing–General Dynamics F-22 Lightning II had been frozen, making the F-22 of 2002 shorter front-to-back and lower on its landing gear, while giving it more wingspan than the YF-22A, selected as the U.S. Air Force's next-generation air superiority fighter.

The F-22's external design freeze, approved by the U.S. Air Force on 31 December 1991, will allow construction of both wind tunnel and radar cross section models as well as revision of its internal design and preparations for full production of the aircraft.

Many of the design alterations are intended to reduce the fighter's radar cross section, and to improve its already excellent

A YF-22 flies in formation with a YF-23 near Edwards Air Force Base, California, circa late 1990. The Northrop–McDonnell Douglas YF-23, unofficially dubbed Grey Ghost, *featured outboard-canted tail planes that doubled as horizontal and vertical stabilizers to provide pitch (nose-up–nose-down) and yaw (nose-left–nose-right) while also providing excellent stability. U.S. Air Force; Tony Landis*

maneuverability in subsonic, transonic, and supersonic speed regimes. The latter is important, as it will permit the F-22 to be pointed rapidly in the direction in which the pilot desires to launch a missile or fire the cannon.

The major external changes include these:

● Increased the wingspan from 43 feet to 44 feet, 6 inches for a better aspect ratio and improved subsonic cruise efficiency.

● Decreased the leading edge wing sweepback from 48 degrees on the YF-22A to 42 degrees on the F-22 of 2002. This alteration is to improve maneuverability.

● Changed all other perimeter edges to the same sweepback angle as that on the wing leading edge—42 degrees—to improve the F-22's radar cross section.

● Decreased the wing root

This concept for an Advanced Tactical Fighter production line depicts some of the manufacturing advances being developed at Lockheed. Extensive use of robotics, paperless processes, and interchangeable tooling, completely integrated by computer, will increase quality and reduce production costs. Such a factory environment will also feature greater flexibility, with increased capability for production surges. Lockheed planners say these technologies, combined with the introduction of new composite materials, will permit production of F-22 fighters with unprecedented quality and durability. Lockheed; Syd Mead

thickness from that of the YF-22A to reduce drag, and modified the wing camber and twist to improve supersonic maneuverability.

• Reduced the vertical tail surfaces from 109 square feet each to 89 square feet each, resulting in less weight and drag and reduced height without loss of control efficiency.

• Reduced the height of the landing gear to lower aircraft height from 17 feet, 7 inches on the YF-22A to 16 feet, 5 inches on the final version.

• Moved the engine air intake lip aft 18 inches to reduce weight and enhance stability and control.

• Reconfigured the trailing edges of the horizontal tail surfaces, but retained the same 68 square foot area on either side.

• Shortened the overall length from the YF-22A's 64 feet, 2 inches to the final version's 62 feet, 1 inch.

• Made the nose section blunter for radar cross section-reduction reasons, and moved the cockpit forward for improved over-the-nose pilot visibility.

When and if the U.S. Air Force gets the F-22, the F-15's long reign will be over. Yet, from all early indications, the Skunk Works–designed F-22 will be a worthy replacement. And, if the name

If all goes well, Lockheed will also produce a navalized version of its F-22 *to replace the Grumman F-14 Tomcat.* Lockheed; Syd Mead

Lightning II survives, it will be a fitting tribute to Kelly Johnson, designer of the original Lightning and founder of the Skunk Works.

YF-22A Specifications

Type	Single-seat service test advanced tactical fighter
Wingspan	43 feet
Wing area	830 square feet (estimated)
Length	64 feet, 2 inches
Height	17 feet, 8³/₄ inches
Empty weight	34,000 pounds (estimated)
Maximum weight	60,000 pounds (estimated)
Maximum speed	Mach 2.5 plus
Service ceiling	60,000 feet (estimated)
Rate of climb	30,000 feet plus (estimated)
Maximum range	Unlimited with aerial refueling
Armament	4 short-range and 4 medium-range air-to-air guided missiles; 1 advanced 20 millimeter General Electric M61 Vulcan cannon
Powerplant	2 Pratt & Whitney YF119-PW-100 (Model PW5000) afterburning 35,000 pound-thrust-class turbofan engines (number 2); 2 General Electric YF120-GE-100 (Model GE37) afterburning 35,000 pound-thrust-class turbofan engines (number 1)

Note: The winning YF-22A number one, and production F-22s, will be powered by the Pratt & Whitney F119 engine. No official name has been announced for future F-22s, but two possible names have been mentioned: Lightning II and Superstar.

YF-22A Production

Designation	Serial Number	Comments
YF-22A	N22YF	Stored, minus engines, at U.S. Air Force Plant 6, Marietta, Georgia
YF-22A	N22YX	Winner of fly-off; issued serial number 87-700; crashed 25 April 1992

Note: Respectively, YF-22As number one and two originally carried civil registration numbers N22YF and N22YX; YF-22A number two, however, was purchased by the U.S. Air Force and received U.S. Air Force serial number 87-700. The General Electric YF120–powered YF-22A, minus its engines, in 1992, was being stored at U.S. Air Force Plant 6 (Lockheed) Marietta, Georgia; no determination has been made as to its disposition. Likewise, since its crash, no determination has been made to the disposition of the Pratt & Whitney YF119–powered YF-22A—winner of the advanced tactical fighter contest.

Postscript

From its rudimentary beginnings a half century ago to its current challenges—classified, naturally—the Lockheed Skunk Works has quietly and quickly designed, developed, and built a number of the world's most prestigious and elusive aircraft. Many of which remain unmentionable. Some of which will never be discussed. And who knows what it might have out there at this writing?

For example, rumors of *Aurora* have—and do—run rampant. Supposedly, *Aurora* is a very high altitude, very high speed reconnaissance air vehicle optimized to replace the retired SR-71. Whether such an advanced aircraft actually exists, however, remains to be seen. But if it does, it likely is a product of the Skunk Works. For when it is asked to produce, it does, in record time and under budget.

Expert management, dynamic engineering, and spellbinding aircraft are the essence of the Skunk Works.

On 24 August 1992, while outlining the evolution of the F-22 advanced tactical fighter, in delivering the 1992 Wright Brothers Lecture at Hilton Head, South Carolina, to the AIAA, Lockheed Advanced Development Company president Sherm Mullin emphasized the need to take risks in order to achieve significant advances.

Presented yearly, the Wright Brothers Lectures on Aeronautics commemorates the first powered flights made by Orville and Wilbur Wright in 1903 at Kitty Hawk, South Carolina. Each lecture is intended to emphasize significant advances in aeronautics by recognizing major leaders and their contributions.

Mullin, who previously directed the Lockheed-Boeing-General Dynamics team effort as vice president and general manager, Advanced Tactical Fighter programs, for Lockheed Aeronautical Systems Company stated in part:

"It was a great privilege to lead the Lockheed-Boeing-General Dynamics team that successfully integrated a wide array of new technology into the F-22, winning the competition to develop the Advanced Tactical Fighter for the U.S. Air Force.

"The F-22 is a truly revolutionary airplane, designed in a unique team environment. We succeeded because we were willing to take the necessary technical risks."

276

"Aeronautical engineering was not meant to be a profession obsessed with very low risk. Increasing numbers of engineers are averse to risk, are greatly impeding our efforts. They remain a major obstacle to future aeronautical engineering accomplishments in the form of new airplanes with very unique capabilities.

"In the case of the F-22 we knowingly took on an enormous system integration challenge to combine supercruise, low observability, integrated avionics and classic fighter performance in a new airplane.

"The ATF was one of the last major opportunities of this century and we met the challenge. The question is whether we will continue to do so in aeronautics. There is no such thing as a low risk future program in aeronautics. We have unlimited opportunities as we march into the 21st century but we must continue in the tradition of the Wright Brothers or we will slowly wither away."

The Skunk Works, founded in mid-1943, has always taken technical risks. This has been proved for fifty years. No one knows what the Skunk Works will generate in the next half century.

One thing is for sure: it will be unique!

During fiscal year 1954, Lockheed's Skunk Works produced five new-build RB-69As for gathering electronic intelligence (serial numbers 54-4037 through 54-404); two others (54-4042 and 54-4043) were created from a pair of modified Navy P2V-7 airframes. Af-ter Lockheed's U-2 entered service in 1956, these seven Neptunes were transferred to the Navy as P2V-7Us, and later, were modified to SP-2H standard. A hush-hush program, little is known about RB-69A activities. Lockheed

A family portrait of Lockheed black jets. In the foreground is an F-117A; in the background is an SR-71A; and in the middle is a U-2R. Three very different aircraft for three very different missions. Lockheed via Tony Landis

In the early 1960s, to obtain air density measurements at altitudes up to 1,000,000 feet for the X-15 research program, a high-altitude research rocket was suspended from the belly of an F-104A (56-0749) on a special retractable trapeze-type launcher that was designed by Kelly Johnson. The rocket had a balloon in its nose that was designed to inflate at a predetermined altitude and its descent rate was measured by radar. The rocket, a sled track rocket modified with fins for guidance and a nose cone to house the balloon, was launched by project pilots at up to 60,000 feet while in a vertical climb. This same launching mechanism was tested by the U.S. Air Force for aerial launchings of the Douglas AIR-2 Genie, an air-to-air nuclear missile, used by the U.S. Air Force's Aerospace Defense Command. NASA

NASA drawing shows high-altitude research rocket leaving the launch rack of a NASA research F-104 while in a vertical climb. The program was flown by NASA project pilots at Edwards Air Force Base in the early 1960s. Unfor- tunately, in December 1962, the actual test F-104A (56-0749) was destroyed in a crash. Whether it was due to the aforementioned rocket-firing tests remains unclear. NASA

Kelly Johnson poses with his most famous creation—the Lockheed Black-bird. Lockheed

In 1983, Kelly Johnson receives one of two medals awarded to him from President Reagan—the National Security

Medal, and in 1988, the National Medal of Technology. Lockheed

A 1978 portrait of Kelly Johnson by
George Wilson. Lockheed

Ben Rich poses with the fifty-ninth and last production F-117A. Leading the development of the F-117A, Rich won the 1989 Collier Trophy in association with the entire Lockheed—U.S. Air Force team responsible for the success of the stealth fighter program. Lockheed

Bibliography

Blay, Roy. "Lockheed X-7 Ramjet Vehicle." *Lockheed Horizons Magazine* (Lockheed Corporation, Burbank, CA) 19 (1985).

Brown, Buddy L. *The Dragon Lady Pilots.* Unclassified document. Unknown date of publication.

Davis, Larry. *P-80 Shooting Star T-33/ F-94 in Action.* Carrollton, TX: Squadron/Signal Publications, 1980.

Drendel, Lou. *SR-71 Blackbird in Action.* Carrollton, TX: Squadron/Signal Publications, 1982.

Francillon, Rene J. *Lockheed Aircraft Since 1913.* Annapolis, MD: Naval Institute Press, 1987.

Francillon, Rene J., and Keaveney, Kevin. *Lockheed F-94 Starfire.* Aerofax Minigraph 14. Arlington, TX: Aerofax, 1986.

Johnson, Clarence L. "Development of the Lockheed SR-71 Blackbird." *Lockheed Horizons Magazine* (Lockheed Corporation, Burbank, CA) (Winter 1981–82).

Johnson, Clarence L., with Smith, Maggie. *Kelly: More Than My Share of It All.* Washington, D.C.: Smithsonian Institution Press, 1985.

Kinzey, Bert. *F-104 Starfighter in Detail and Scale.* Vol. 38. Blue Ridge Summit, PA: TAB/McGraw-Hill Books, 1991.

"Lockheed-California Company, Skunk Works Programs." *Lockheed Horizons Magazine* (Lockheed Corporation, Burbank, CA) 12 (1983).

Lockheed Corporation. *We Own the Night.* Calabasas, CA: Lockheed Creative Communications, 1992.

"Lockheed SR-71 Supersonic/Hypersonic Research Facility." *Researcher's Handbook.* Vol. 1, *Executive Summary.* Sunland, CA: Lockheed Advanced Development Company, 1992.

McIninch, Thomas P. *The OXCART Story.* Unclassified document number SC-86-010115. 1986.

Miller, Jay. *Lockheed SR-71 (A-12/ YF-12/D-21).* Aerofax Minigraph 1. Arlington, TX: Aerofax, 1985.

Miller, Jay. *The X-Planes X-1 to X-31.* Revised Edition. Arlington, TX: Aerofax for Orion Books, 1988.

"Operation Desert Storm, Stealth, Our Role in the Gulf." *Lockheed Magazine* (Lockheed Creative Communications, Calabasas, CA) 3, no. 1 (June 1991).

Pace, Steve. *F-117A Stealth Fighter.* Aero Series, vol. 43. Blue Ridge Summit, PA: TAB/McGraw-Hill Books, 1992.

Pace, Steve. *Lockheed F-104 Starfighter.* Osceola, WI: Motorbooks International Publishers and Wholesalers, 1992.

Pace, Steve. *X-Fighters: U.S. Air Force Experimental and Prototype Fighters, XP-59 to YF-23.* Osceola, WI: Motorbooks International Publishers and Wholesalers, 1991.

"Secret First Flight of Article 001." *Spyplanes Magazine* (Challenge Publications, Canoga Park, CA) 2 (1988).

Sweetman, Bill, and Goodall, James. *Lockheed F-117A.* Osceola, WI: Motorbooks International Publishers and Wholesalers, 1990.

This Is . . . LADC. Lockheed pamphlet. Sunland, CA: Lockheed Advanced Development Company Employee Communications, 1991.

Thornborough, Anthony M., and Davies, Peter E. *Lockheed Blackbirds.* Shepperton, Surrey, England: Ian Allan, 1988.

Index

9th Strategic Reconnaissance Wing, 201
37th Tactical Fighter Wing, 241, 244-246
49th Fighter Wing, 244, 246, 253
319th Fighter All Weather Squadron, 76
415th Fighter Squadron, 238, 246
416th Fighter Squadron, 238, 246
417th Fighter Squadron, 238, 246
4200th Test Wing, 180
4450th Tactical Group, 233, 245, 252
4450th Test Squadron, 238
4451st Test Squadron, 238
4453rd Test and Evaluation Squadron, 238

A-7D Corsair II, 238
A-11, 156-158, 202
A-12, 19, 153-182, 186, 201-203, 205, 216
Adana, Turkey, 164
Advanced Tactical Fighter, 254, 273, 276
Aeromite Mighty Mouse, 80
Aerospace Defense Command, 183, 189
Agena-D satellite, 15
AIM-9 Sidewinder, 263, 265
AIM-120, 265
Air Materiel Command, 59, 85, 87, 94
Allen, James S., 235, 255
Allis-Chalmers' J36 Goblin engine, 51
Allison company, 59, 63, 65-66, 73-75, 77, 119, 123
Ames/Dryden Flight Research Facility, 195, 211
AN/APA-84 computer, 80
AN/APG-33 radar, 73, 77
AN/APG-40 radar, 77
AN/ARN-5B, 77
AN/ARN-12 receiver, 76
AN/ASG-18 radar, 183, 185
Andre, Colonel Daniel, 192
Arnold, General Henry H. ("Hap"), 42
Aurora, 276

B-17 Flying Fortress, 44, 114
B-29 Superfortress, 98, 101
B-52H Stratofortress, 180
B-57 Canberra, 131
B-58 Hustler, 227
B-70 Valkyrie, 136
Baldwin, Ed, 107
Beale Air Force Base, 137, 180, 201, 205, 209
Beesley, Jon, 265, 268

Bell Aircraft Corporation, 35, 43, 131, 133
Benson, H. L., 52
Betz, Stanley, 123
Bison, W.L., 52
Bissell, Richard M., 153
Black Shield, 173-174, 176, 178
Blackburn Aircraft, 246
Boehme, Dick, 52, 107
Boeing company, 20, 121, 123, 254, 260, 271-272, 276
Bohacek, L. J., 52
Bohn-Meyer, Marta, 212
Bojens, H. R., 52
Bong, Major Richard I., 55
Bradley, A., 52
Bristow, Guy, 48
Brotherton, Lt. Cmdr. Michael, 121
Brown, Alan, 245-246, 249
Brown, G. F., 52
Burcham, Milo, 41, 49-50, 55

C-130 Hercules, 121, 124, 163
C-140A JetStar, 128
Canadair, 61, 65
Cannestra, Ken, 31
Cantrell, C. R. ("Dick"), 245-246, 250
Capp, Al, 11
Central Intelligence Agency, 131, 133-136, 153-154, 156, 162, 165, 167-168, 176, 180, 197, 199-201, 206
China Lake Naval Weapons Center, 263
Clifford, Clark M., 206
Collins, Kenneth, 167, 180
Colman, Philip A., 36, 38, 107, 134
Combs, Henry, 107
Constellation, 107, 114
Convair, 113, 117, 119, 154, 183, 189
Cooney, Major James P., 192
CP-140, 111
Cuban Missile Crisis, 166
Culver, Irving H. ("Irv"), 43-44, 52
Curtiss-Wright Corporation, 38, 70, 121

D-21 Drone, 164, 180-182
Daniel, Lieutenant Colonel Walter F., 192
Daniell, Rus, 73, 81, 107
Danielson, H. C., 52
de Havilland, 9, 35, 43, 48

Defense Advanced Research Projects Agency, 222
Delmer, General Marvin, 185
Douglas Aircraft, 70, 121, 123, 134, 172
Dryden Flight Research Facility, 127
Dulles International Airport, 209
Dyson, Lieutenant Colonel Norman Kenneth ("Ken"), 224-225

Eastham, James D. ("Jim"), 187, 193
Edwards Air Force Base, 11, 48, 72, 82, 94, 118-119, 122-123, 126, 136, 161, 169, 175, 184, 187-188, 250, 259, 262, 265, 271, 279
Eglin Army Air Field, 39, 42
Eielson Air Force Base, 164
Eisenhower, President Dwight D., 130, 154-155
Estes, Jr., Brigadier General Howell M., 185

F-12, 187, 189, 192
F-22, 20, 238, 250, 254-276
F-80 Shooting Star, 9, 11, 22, 39-54, 55, 58, 61, 64, 66, 70, 75, 82, 114, 134
F-86 Sabre, 104
F-90, 114
F-94 Starfire, 15, 53, 65-84, 114
F-104 Starfighter, 19, 22, 80, 104, 111, 134, 163, 278
F-105 Thunderchief, 168
F-117 Stealth Fighter, 20, 22, 24, 225, 227-254, 259, 283
F3D Skyknight, 75
Fairchild, 121, 123, 131, 133
Farley, Harold C. ("Hal"), 228, 234
Federal Aviation Administration, 163
Ferguson, David L. ("Dave"), 228, 259, 262
Fife, Edward, 52
Flock, Art, 117
Frost, Eugene C. ("Gene"), 38, 107, 134
Fulkerson, Glen, 72, 74, 82

General Dynamics company, 20, 154, 186, 189, 224, 235, 254, 260, 268, 270-272, 276
General Electric company, 35, 51, 255
General Electric engines, 35, 51, 77, 80, 108, 111, 133, 183, 222, 260, 262, 265, 267
Gilliland, Robert J. ("Bob"), 187, 200-201
Goodyear, 113
Gordon, Jack, 245-246, 248
Gossett, G. W., 52
Grey Ghost, 50-51
Groom Lake test site, 131, 161, 186, 224
Gross, Robert E., 26, 42
Grumman, 65, 189, 254, 260, 274

Halford, Major Frank B., 48
Harris, Lawrence M., 254
Haughton, Daniel, 174
Have Blue, 219, 222-225, 227, 254
Hawkins, Willis M., 37-38, 107
Heinkel, 31
Helms, Richard, 176, 199-200, 206
Heppe, R. Richard ("Dick"), 107, 111, 134
Hibbard, Hall L., 33, 42, 52, 58, 107
Hill, D. C., 52
Hiller Helicopters, 119
Hirth, 31
Holbury, Colonel Robert J., 163
Holland, R. L., 52
Holloman Air Force Base, 245-246
Holloway, Colonel Bruce, 107
Holm, Skip, 228
Hong, James, 111
Howard, Dan, 235
Hughes, 77, 183, 186, 189, 192

J31 jet engine, 35
J33 jet engine, 59, 63, 65-66, 73-75, 77, 119, 123
J34 jet engine, 80
J36 jet engine, 35
J48 jet engine, 77, 82
J58 jet engine, 156, 162
J75 jet engine, 137, 163, 166
Jackson, Colonel Robert A., 233
Johnson, Clarence L. ("Kelly"), 9, 11, 14-15, 18-19, 22-23, 26-27, 32, 38-40, 44, 48-49, 51-53, 66, 73, 86, 94, 102, 104-107, 113, 117, 121, 126, 132, 145, 154-155, 159, 162, 165, 174, 176, 192, 207, 278, 280-282

Kadena Air Force Base, 164, 173, 176, 178
Kammerer, Dorsey, 48
Kawasaki, 61, 65
KC-10 Extender, 243
KC-135 Stratotanker, 204, 207
Kelly Johnson Research and Development Center, 18, 28
Kentucky Air National Guard, 121
Kerr, J. F., 53
Kirkham, R. L., 53

L-1000 axialflow turbojet engine, 32
L-1011, 111, 249
LADC Information Sheet, 30
Langley Air Force Base, 246
Layton, Ronald J., 180
Le Vier, Anthony W. ("Tony"), 40, 45, 48, 51, 59, 62, 67, 71, 74, 82, 88, 92, 94, 104, 106, 134-135
Ledford, Brigadier General Jack C., 173, 175

286

Li'l Abner, 11
Lockheed company, 62, 121-122, 133, 168, 254, 272, 276
Lulu-Belle, 11, 15, 40, 48-50, 61
Lux, David P., 212

Marquardt company, 86
Marquardt, R. F., 96
Martin company, 96, 113, 131
Mayaguez, 138
McChord Air Force Base, 76
McCone, John, 165-166, 173
McDonnell Douglas company, 20, 87, 90, 163, 180, 235, 240, 254, 260-261, 270, 272, 274
McIninch, Thomas P., 162
McLane, P. W., 53
McNamara, Robert S., 173, 187, 189
Menasco Manufacturing Company, 38
Mikoyan MiG, 104-105
Model 10 Electra, 14, 114
Model 14 Super Electra, 15
Model 580, 58-60
Model 780, 73
Model 880, 77
Model 1080, 63
Morgenfeld, Tom, 260, 265-266
Moses Lake Air Force Base, 76
Moss, V. D., 53
Mulhare, Major Ross E., 235, 252
Mullin, Sherman N. ("Sherm"), 9, 20, 22-23, 30, 276
Muroc Army Air Field, 11, 15, 45, 48, 51, 92
Muroc Dry Lake, 49
Murray, Francis J., 180

NAS Moffett Field, 140
NASA, 127, 138, 190, 211, 214, 217, 279
Nellis Air Force Base, 134, 154, 175, 180, 186, 224-225, 227, 229, 235, 238, 240
Nelson, Norm, 245-247, 251
North American Air Defense Command (NORAD), 163
North American company, 58, 65, 85, 109, 136, 175, 183-184, 224
Northrop company, 20, 66-67, 75, 77, 109, 113, 222, 224, 235, 238, 254, 259-260
Nunn, Sam, 18

Operation Desert Storm, 24, 237, 246
OXCART, 155, 158, 162, 164, 166, 168, 170, 172, 175, 178, 180, 184-185, 196, 201, 203, 206

P-2 Neptune, 15
P-3 Orion, 20, 22, 114

P-38 Lightning, 14, 39, 41, 85, 114
P-47 Thunderbolt, 85
P-59 Airacomet, 39, 43
P-80 Shooting Star, 39, 41, 52, 55, 59, 66, 96-97
P-Unit, 4451st Test Squadron, 238
P2V-7, 277
Pacific Missile Test Center, 264
Packard, David, 18
Palmer, Don, 44, 53, 58, 86
Parangosky, John, 174
Park, William M. ("Bill"), 146, 171, 173, 175, 224
Perkins, Dr. Courtlandt, 185
Peterson, Art, 146
Powell, Colonel Robert M., 209
Powers, Lieutenant Francis Gary ("Frank"), 130, 136, 153
Pratt & Whitney company, 77, 133, 136, 155-156, 162, 168, 208, 216, 255, 260, 265, 270-271
Price, Nathan C. ("Nate"), 31-32
Project Bald Eagle, 130, 133
Project GUSTO, 153-155
Project MX-409, 44
Project MX-883, 97
Project Senior Bowl, 179
Project Senior Crown, 196, 201, 207
Putt, General Donald L. ("Don"), 107

Ralston, William P. ("Bill"), 44, 53, 86, 107
Ranch, the, 134
Ray, Walter, 175
RB-69A, 277
RC-105D localizer receiver, 77
Reconnaissance Star, 138
Rempt, Henry F., 53
Republic, 85
Rich, Benjamin R., 18, 29, 107, 142, 219, 227, 244, 283
Riedenauer, Robert L., 233
RJ30-MA-1, 96
Rockwell, 254, 260
Rogers Dry Lake, 11, 49, 72, 92
Rolls-Royce Tay, 77
Roth, Colonel Marshall S., 39, 42
Rye Canyon Research Laboratory, 28

S-3 Viking, 20, 111
Salmon, Herman R. ("Herm" or "Fish"), 82, 97, 110, 113-114, 116, 118
Schackelford, Major Mark, 268
Schalk, Louis ("Lou"), 165, 177, 187
Schroeder, Bill, 221
Schultze, George, 199, 201
Senior Bowl, 179

Senior Crown, 196, 201, 207
Senior Trend, 225, 229
Short, Mac V.F., 55
Silver Ghost, 50-51
Slater, Colonel Hugh C., 176, 180
Smithsonian Institution, 209
SNJ trainer aircraft, 58
Solar company, 92
SR-71 Blackbird, 15, 21-22, 184-185, 196-218, 250, 254, 276
Supersonic Transport (SST), 111
Stadler, Rich, 153
Stearman, W. M., 53
Stephens, Colonel Robert L., 192
Stewart, Michael C., 235, 253
Strategic Air Command, 107, 166, 199-201, 205-206, 209
Stroud, John, 107
Sullivan, Dennis B., 179-180
Swoffard, Lieutenant Colonel Ralph, 44
Sylvanus Albert Reed Awards, 18
Szep, Joe, 53

T-1A SeaStar, 61, 63-65
T-6 Texan, 58
T-33, 15, 53, 55-65, 114, 119
Tactical Air Command, 227, 245
Taylor, Vice-Admiral Rufus L., 180
TDN L-188, 77
TF-80C Shooting Star, 60, 67, 74-75
Thule Air Base, 164
Titanium Metals Corporation, 158
TO-1, 66, 75
TO-2, 60
Tolin, Colonel Anthony J. ("Tony"), 238, 241
Tonopah Test Range, 237, 239-241
Torick, Ray, 179
TP-80C, 59, 66, 70, 73
TR-1, 142
TR-1A, 138-139
TR-1B, 138-139
TV-2, 60-61

U-2, 9, 19, 22, 130-154, 173, 175, 250
U.S. Far East Air Force, 107
United Aircraft Corporation, 155, 166
UV-1, 128

V-J Day, 39, 52
Vance, Cyrus R., 173, 199, 201
Vida, Lieutenant Colonel Joseph T., 209-210
Vierick, Arthur M. ("Art"), 44, 48, 53, 107
Vojvodich, Mele, 171, 180

Warner, Major Noel T., 12
Weeks, Jack W., 180, 206
Westinghouse engines, 52, 54, 92
White Sands Proving Ground, 100
Wilson, George, 282
Wimmer, Roy, 123
Wright Aeronautical, 38
Wright Army Air Field, 39, 42
Wright-Patterson Air Force Base, 185, 194, 227, 255

X-7, 96-103
X-31A, 224
X-104, 16
XF-87 Blackhawk, 66
XF-88 Voodoo, 92, 94
XF-90, 54, 85-95, 111
XF-93A, 94
XF-104 Starfighter, 80, 104-112, 132
XF3D-1 Skyknight, 70
XFV-1 Salmon, 113-120
XJ37 jet engine, 38
XP-80 Shooting Star, 11, 14-15, 22, 40, 42-44, 48, 50-51, 53-54
XP-88 Voodoo, 90-91
XQ-5 King Fisher, 96-103
XST, 219-226

Yates, General Don, 107
YC-103, 111
YC-130 Hercules, 121
Yeilding, Lieutenant Colonel Edward, 210
YF-12 Blackbird, 168, 183-195, 205, 216, 254
YF-22 Advanced Tactical Fighter, 20, 256, 270
YF-23A Advanced Tactical Fighter, 20, 260, 264-265
YF-94 Starfire, 71-75, 77, 82-84
YF-97A, 80
YF-104A Starfighter, 114
York, A. J., 53
YP-80A Shooting Star, 41, 52
YT40-A-6 turboprop engine, 118